ESCAPE

THE FOUR STAGES OF BECOMING
A SUCCESSFUL ENTREPRENEUR

ANIK SINGAL

Lurn, Inc.
2098 Gaither Road
Rockville, MD 20850
www.lurn.com
ISBN-13: 978-0-9972079-5-8

DEDICATION

I always find this to be one of the hardest parts of writing a book.

There are so many amazing people in my life who've inspired me throughout my Entrepreneurial journey. There are so many who have mentored me. Most importantly, there are so many who have supported me through both the good times and the bad - without you, I wouldn't still be standing.

Although I couldn't possibly name everyone, I want to do my best to recognize all of the people who have made it possible for me to chase and achieve my dreams.

To God:
Years ago, you handed me a purpose and told me to go forth. It was like someone handing me a brand new life. Since then, you've provided me with all of the support that I've needed to help myself grow both as a person and as a professional. I'm constantly in awe of how you break down my obstacles and remove all hurdles. I'm blessed that you chose me for this mission. Thank you.

To my parents, Balwant and Anita Singal:
I feel like I have an unfair advantage in life with you as my parents. You've taught me what true love is, the value of hard work, how to be persistent and how to always strive to be the best. Mom, Dad, you're the best. Thank you so much for all that you've done for me.

To my amazing wife, Andrea:
I'm amazed at how you put up with my craziness on a regular basis. It's no wonder that my entire life turned around the day you said "yes" to marrying me. It's not luck; it's design. You were what I needed to truly complete my life. Thank you for always standing strong beside me. Thank you for always taking care of me. Most of all, thank you for loving me and supporting me no matter what.

To my sister and brother-in-law, Kazal & Pyush Bahl:
I think back to when I was sick in the hospital for weeks and months. Not a moment went by when you weren't by my side. I know what you both have sacrificed in your lives to support me. Thank you so much. You are truly the best siblings I could have wished for. With you, I know one thing - someone always has my back.

To my crazy nephews, Ronak & Niam Bahl:
From the 9:00 p.m. Facetime calls where we have "silly face" competitions to the moments when you scream in excitement when you see your uncle go on stage, you two are a true inspiration to me. I am inspired to think that you may look at me as a role model one day. You two make me laugh more than anyone in the world.

To my rambunctious family in India – Colin, Letty, Abigail & Tania:
I can feel your prayers all the way from India. Thank you for all you do for me. Thank you for always making me smile when life is tough. Thank you for always showing me just how lively life can be. Thank you for constantly reminding me what *really* matters in life.

To my Gucci Gang group of friends – Jimmy, Jon, Fred, Dan, Rito & Ratan:
I remember watching *Good Will Hunting* once and being jealous of Matt Damon's friends. They would do anything for him. They always had his back. Today, I realize that I got exactly what I wished for. No matter what it is, when it is, or what it requires, you guys always support me and lift me up. Thank you.

To my Lurn team:
I don't even know where to start. From my mood swings and crazy ideas to the sleepless nights and long weekends, you never leave my side. Your support, your brilliance, and your dedication to our collective purpose inspire me every waking moment of my life. Thank you for always working so hard for our #LurnNation.

To my mentors – Solomon Evangelista, Justin Ford, Scott Laughlin, Shambo, Ian & Naomi Hendricks & Jean-Pierre Leblanc
I am forever grateful for the time you've invested in helping me become the person I want to be. I will never be able to repay you all for your

kindness, but I work hard every day and night just to make you proud. Thank you so much for always giving to me so selflessly. I promise I'll always pay it forward in your name.

To anyone I've ever met:
I can honestly say that I want to dedicate this book to every single person I've ever met in my life. Even if it was just a 10-second conversation, you've in some way impacted my life and led me to writing this book. Thank you.

To all you ENTREPRENEURS:
I read your crazy stories from all over the world. Here's to your huge dreams, ridiculous visions, and relentless persistence. You all inspire me every day of my life. In the end, I have you to thank the most because I never would have started my journey as an Entrepreneur without all of you.

So, I dedicate this book to all of you incredible people.

Thank you for everything you've done for me in my life. I only pray that I get the chance to repay your debt.

Sincerely,
Anik Singal

TABLE OF CONTENTS

FOREWORD
BY DAYMOND JOHN

I've been an entrepreneur all my life and have worked with countless other entrepreneurs throughout my career. I can tell you from experience that, when it comes to finding success, it's not about having the right answers. Instead, it's about asking the right questions.

Most entrepreneurs are focused on their idea, their funding, their network and so many other elements. Now, don't get me wrong; these are all important aspects of what makes a successful company. At the same time, these elements are not what *truly* determine the success of a company.

The main focus needs to be on the entrepreneur themselves. Before I built the multi-billion dollar brand FUBU or became a shark on *Shark Tank*, I was just a boy from the Hollis neighborhood in Queens, New York trying to help his family make ends meet.

Whether I was selling pencils, shoveling driveways or working at Red Lobster, I was quietly perfecting all the skills I needed to master in order to succeed as an entrepreneur.

When I'm reviewing pitches inside or outside of The Tank, my number one priority is not the business itself, the revenue, the market share or even profits. The very first thing I focus on is the person behind the presentation. I want to see what they're made of, who they are, how they think and how capable they are of bouncing back.

Think of it this way: there's a very good chance that I might be talking with this entrepreneur way more than I talk with my own family and friends. I need to make sure I'm ready to connect with this person on a regular basis and that I'm excited to pick up the phone and give whatever guidance I can when they call in the middle of the night.

That's why I'm so glad that Anik wrote this book and that all aspiring and established entrepreneurs can focus on the common elements that the most successful entrepreneurs in the world share.

The bottom-line is this: a prepared and trained entrepreneur should be ready to tackle anything. That includes any internal problem, industry shift, customer habit change or any other worldly challenge – it doesn't matter. Before you can handle any of those, the first question that an entrepreneur needs to ask is, "How do I become a prepared and trained entrepreneur?"

That's not an easy question to ask, but this book gives you the blueprint to arrive at that answer.

The traditional systems have raised us to think, feel and act very differently than what is necessary to become a successful entrepreneur. The only way to overwrite that coding is through awareness, practice and guidance.

When Anik asked me to write the foreword to this book, I was excited to have the opportunity to talk directly to entrepreneurs and share a few lessons I've picked up along the way.

Let's get into it:
Three Key Lessons to Becoming a Successful Entrepreneur
Growing up, I didn't have a book like *eSCAPE* to guide me. I wish I did. However, I was very fortunate to have an amazing mother who taught me the following core lessons that allowed me to become the person I am today:

#1 – Think Big, Act Small – Always take affordable steps so your mistakes are never too big to recover from. Be strategic and wise with how you approach a project.

#2 – Make Fast Decisions – The greatest of entrepreneurs can achieve far more than the rest of the world in the same amount of time. This is because of their ability to be decisive and make fast, effective decisions.

#3 – It's All About Execution – Look, there are millions of great ideas out there. I mean, how many times have you had a friend or relative propose a new idea for a product or company? I would bet you that the majority of the time, they rarely move on that concept to make it a reality. The most successful people move and take action.

When I'm sitting down to evaluate a deal on *Shark Tank*, these are the first three qualities I look for in the entrepreneur, *not the business.*

Now, the real question becomes *"how"* do we build the right characteristics, behaviors and patterns in ourselves to succeed as an entrepreneur?

Well, until today, it was a combination of hard work, your network, a decent amount of luck and making those mistakes yourself. However, with this book, Anik gives you a tested formula, and he speeds up that entire process for you so you don't have to waste money, energy and time learning these lessons the hard way.

That's what this book does...

It gives you an entire plan to escape your current life and finally get the one you've always dreamt of. It won't be easy, but at least now you have the formula to follow.

Here's to changing the world.

Daymond John

"The People's Shark"

PREFACE:
ARE YOU READY?

Steve Jobs once said, *"I'm convinced that about half of what separates the successful Entrepreneurs from the non-successful ones is pure perseverance."* It's advice that many of us have heard before. We should be persistent, be consistent, never give up, always hustle and never quit...

But one question keeps coming to mind – *how?*

Is it enough to motivate ourselves with books and seminars, or do we need new tools and skills in our repertoire to make it happen? Is there a way we can make it our natural state to fight and persevere?

Years ago, these questions led me down the path of an amazing journey – a journey to discover what separates a successful Entrepreneur from the unsuccessful. I honestly never expected that the journey would go so deep. I thought I would speak to 10 successful Entrepreneurs and walk away with 10 clear characteristics.

I couldn't have been more wrong.

What I learned is that becoming an Entrepreneur truly requires a different molding. There are stages of growth. There are belief patterns. There are multiple characteristics and differences between what we're taught and how an Entrepreneur actually functions.

Through my research, I discovered my mission in life: to build The Transformational Home for Entrepreneurs. I became obsessed with wanting to build a community that provides training, support and coaching for Entrepreneurs.

This book is the culmination of my research and what I hope becomes the spark that empowers people from all over the world to fight for their dreams. This book truly comes directly from my heart. In it, I provide honest opinions on what it takes to become a successful Entrepreneur.

My goal here is simple.

I want you to have exactly what you want from your life. I want you to break out of the system. I want you to have all the support you need to finally become the Entrepreneur you've always dreamed of being.

I wrote every single word in this book with that exact mentality.

We're about to embark on a life-changing journey, and I'm honored that you've allowed me to join you.

* Raises a Glass *

Here's to all you crazy Entrepreneurs all over the world. Here's to a life of making our dreams come true.

Now, **let's get to work!**

CHAPTER 1:
MY STORY

3rd grade, 9 years old.

I had finished my homework, eaten my snacks and was lying back, enjoying some cartoons, when suddenly the doorbell rang. I knew exactly who it was.

It was my 2nd grade employees who ran my lemonade stand. They had come to deliver a box of cash and coins – my earnings for the day. I ran to the door, grabbed the box and sprinted past my mother, who was clearly growing more and more confused by me every day.

I ran to the bedroom and dumped the cash on my bed. *Just how much had I earned today while watching cartoons, sipping lemonade and eating a brownie?*

$3.60

Subtract out the 50% share that I owed to my profit-sharing employees (they were responsible for their own supplies) and I had made a sweet net profit of $1.80.

This was a daily occurrence for a few months.

That meant I was earning $12.60 per week with my business, which was 57.5% more than my $8.00 per week allowance!

My lemonade stand taught me the first lesson I ever learned as an Entrepreneur: **The difference between earning an allowance and creating an allowance.**

Earning Allowance:
Clean the house. Wash the dishes. Behave well. Finish my homework. Mow the lawn. It wasn't easy. The "man" (my parents) expected a lot from me!

Creating Allowance:
Secure a location for my lemonade stand. Hire two trustworthy employees. Watch cartoons.

As long as I could invest in creating the system up front, the rewards were far greater and required far less work from me in the future. This was a great lesson indeed, but one I quickly forgot as I got sucked into the traditional educational system.

From that first Entrepreneurial moment in my life at the age of nine, it took me another 10 years to finally come back and revisit who I truly was at the core: an Entrepreneur.

So, Why Did It Take So Long?

Clearly, I had motivation. Clearly, I was an action-taker. Clearly, I was pretty clever. It took this long because I was immersed in a system that simply does not recognize Entrepreneurship as a career.

I was never really shown that option. As a child, not once was the word "Entrepreneur" ever mentioned to me in school or at home. I came from an Asian-Indian background, and grew up in a family of engineers, doctors and lawyers.

I was never "told" that I should be a doctor, but my surroundings led to me to making that decision myself because I only ever saw one thing:

"If you become a doctor, you will get all the respect, make all the money, buy nice houses and nice cars. Then everyone will say you're successful."

So I worked hard. I studied day and night. I did everything "by the book" and it even paid off. I got accepted into one of the top pre-medical programs in the world. I was even going to be on a full scholarship. As far as the world knew, I was set. I'd never have to look back.

I was ecstatic, excited, proud, and full of hope. That is, until one fateful morning. One day, in my freshman year of college, my eyes opened but not a single part of my body wanted to move. All I could think was,

Just weeks into my first year of college, this feeling had started to settle in. Running to biology class, chemistry class, and cramming for exams – it suddenly wasn't making any sense.

I was scared, and for the first time I was daring to ask, *"Do I even want to be a doctor?"*

After living this life for a few weeks, I finally realized how out of place I was in my surroundings. I didn't feel like I belonged. Not only was becoming a doctor not exciting anymore, but the entire idea of working for someone else and letting them control my life was starting to plague me.

I was staying up at night, staring at my wall, thinking back to my 3rd grade days when I had the "good life." I kept asking myself the same questions.

Where did I go wrong? How did I make this mistake? Most importantly, how was I going to fix it?

So, It Was Time To Test My Theory...

I had to see if I had what it took to succeed as an Entrepreneur – I needed proof before I threw away a "set life" and full scholarship. So, I decided to join a financial planning firm that paid only on commission. I know it sounds random, but it was one of the best things that ever happened to me.

I became an independent contractor and was certified to sell mutual funds, life insurance, annuities, you name it. That's right, an 18-year-old with $100 to his name was now certified to help people with millions to theirs.

Within months, I had $10 million under my management. I was shocked. I wasn't even at the end of my freshman year and I was already making the same amount I could only dream of making after I graduated college?

I knew then that "the system" was broken.

But the good news was that I had my confirmation. Now, all I needed to do was make my announcement. I needed to tell my parents that I wanted to leave it all and switch to business school.

Luckily, my parents and family were incredibly supportive. They didn't agree with my decision, but they vowed to support me all the way. So that was one big relief, but I wasn't done yet…

Was I really ready to throw it all away?

That question plagued me for weeks. Even after my parents, family, and friends had vowed to support me, I couldn't help but wonder whether I was being wise by taking on all that "risk."

Time To Make A Decision

Switching from pre-med to business school was one of the most difficult decisions I have ever made in my life. The craziest part is that *a turtle helped me make it.*

It was December 30, 2002—the night before New Year's Eve. I was desperate. I was scared. I felt like a deer in headlights. I couldn't make a move. I couldn't sleep at night. I couldn't eat. I had become a zombie.

To do or not to do?

It was all I could think about.

I was petrified of the risk. I was throwing away a "for sure" thing for a "risky, who knows" thing. How could I know I was making the right decision? What would happen if I was wrong?

Well, in my season of inner-torture…

…in came God.

I was so frustrated, scared, and tired that for the first time in my life, I turned to God for a solution. I did the whole shebang, down on my hands and knees at my bedside.

"God, if you're there, I need your help. Make this decision for me. Tomorrow night is New Year's Eve. At the stroke of midnight, give me a sign. Tell me what to do!"

Well, there I had it – it was no longer my problem. I just had to wait for my sign.

The next day came and I actually forgot all about my prayer. For New Year's Eve, I was down the street at a friend's house, but I wasn't really in a celebratory mood. I made it to just 10 minutes past the midnight marker and decided to go home.

In Comes The Turtle...

I was just turning into my neighborhood when suddenly I had to jerk my car because something was in the middle of the intersection. I pulled up right next to it, opened the door, and you guessed it...

A giant turtle, easily two feet in length, was sitting right in the middle of the intersection.

Now, know this - I had lived in that neighborhood for more than 10 years. I knew every nook and cranny of that place. I knew every inch of the woods around us and yes, I had seen turtles, but never one even close to this size.

I sat in my car in the middle of the intersection, completely confused. *How did he get here? Why is he so big? What the heck is going on?* After 30 seconds, I decided I had bigger problems in my life and let it be. It was time to go home.

I drove just 100 yards and pulled into my garage. As I pulled in, I got worried about the turtle. He was in a horrible place on one of the biggest drinking holidays of the year.

What if he got hit by a drunk driver? Maybe I should move him?

I ran out towards the intersection to find him, and, well, nothing.

It couldn't have been more than three minutes between the time I had seen the turtle in my car and the time I had returned to pick him up. Only three minutes...

...and the last time I checked, turtles didn't exactly move very fast.

I looked around for five minutes. I walked in every direction and found nothing. I finally gave up, wrote it off to the mysteries of the world, and walked back into the house.

Now this was when my jaw dropped to the ground.

As I walked in, there was a yellow envelope on the kitchen table with a yellow sticky note on it that said, "Time to make a decision." I instantly knew what it was, and I didn't want to open it. I knew that my deadline to decide whether I wanted to go to business school or not was fast approaching.

I picked up the envelope and slowly began pulling out the packet. There it was, staring me in the face – a big terrapin on the cover of the folder sent to me by the University of Maryland, College Park.

It just so turned out that the mascot of the very school that I was debating attending was a turtle. Had I just received the sign that I prayed for? Who knows, but that moment certainly changed my life.

The next day I woke up confident, refreshed, and energetic. I was convinced that I had received the sign to make my decision. I walked downstairs and signed the paperwork. I was going to study business. I was officially on the road to becoming an Entrepreneur!

...or was I?

Fast forward a year to business school. I was attending the classes I always wanted. I was taking classes in advanced marketing, financial management, statistics, human resources, and many other amazing topics. Yet...

...I still hated it!

What the heck was wrong with me? I had made the greatest leap of faith of my life and here I was, still unhappy? Did I just hate school? Was I destined to be a drop-out?

Luckily, I discovered quickly that my problem wasn't with going to classes. My problem was not being able to take action afterwards.

I was hungry for experiential learning. I wanted to start a business. I wanted to take the plunge. I didn't want to wait to graduate and "get a job." I wanted to seize the day and pave my own path immediately.

I only hated school because I was tired of waiting to start the fight for my dreams. I was tired of waiting for someone else's approval that it was okay to start chasing my goals.

The Night I Turned To Google For Help

I knew there had to be an answer to my dilemma, so I turned to the only thing I could think of — Google. Google knows everything, right? I searched, "how to make money." And it was my eureka moment.

It was the moment I was introduced to the idea that people could make money online.

I spent days searching online for something that would work for me. I saw so many business "ideas" and most of them were flat-out scams. I really wasn't sure what to do. I was just about to give up when suddenly I found a great resource that would soon change my life.

It was a forum FULL of real people who were creating online businesses from their home computers, sitting in their pajamas in their basements.

I was intrigued, to say the least. But was it real?

I became active in the forum. I invested hours talking to people. I asked question after question, and they even labeled me as the most annoying kid in the forum. I learned more and more every day. The more I studied, the more excited I grew. It seemed like such a simple system. People were literally sitting with laptops, creating quick websites and making more money per year than most doctors could.

I thought, *"Hey, I can do that!"*

Well, that is until I started trying...

Eighteen months and 50 failures later, I was fed up. Every man has a breaking point and I had finally found mine. I was done. I wanted to quit, give up, and just do what everyone else does - focus on school and get a "good" job.

But before I gave up all my dreams, I figured I'd give it one final go – even though I had zero faith that it would work. I went to the forum and posted this:

I'm quitting in 24 hours – I give up.

Everyone, thank you so much for your help over these many months. The truth is, I've tried and tried and nothing is working. I know it's real. I just don't think it's for me anymore. I haven't made any profit in over a year. I'll give it another 24 hours. If I don't make any money, I'm done. Thank you again to everyone here. I'll miss you guys.

Who knew that one post would change my life for ever?

The First Success... The Night That Changed Everything

I had made my decision to quit and planned to stick to it, but then everything changed the minute I got a private message from a mystery person. To this day, I have no idea who this person was.

They had no post history on the forum and had never messaged me before.

All they said was that they had been watching me for a year and didn't want to see me quit. They said that for the next 24 hours, I could ask for as much help as I wanted. I could message them as much as I needed.

Well, I was skeptical and almost said no.

Thankfully, I decided to give it a shot. So, for hours to come I used every minute of this stranger's time. I don't know why, but I felt good. It felt nice to finally have someone who was helping me. I felt like I actually had a chance!

I banged away at the laptop until at least 3:00 a.m. I didn't sleep until my head was literally bobbing up and down. I did everything I possibly could and then finally threw in the towel.

It was time to see what the future held for me. Would it work?

I remember my eyes opening six hours later. I jolted out of bed and almost tripped and hit my head on the desk. I had to see if it worked. Well, seconds later, I sat with my jaw on the ground…

There it was. **I had just made my first $300!**

My life, as I knew it, would never be the same – ever again.

The Spark That Created My First Empire

That was it — I never looked back from that first $300.

You see, now I had a system. I finally had a simple series of steps that actually worked. Every time I did them, I got results. Everything had become much simpler!

I rinsed and repeated the system over and over. The more I did it, the more my business grew. It almost felt like the blink of an eye that I was able to take my business from that first night of $300 to doing over $10 million a year - all in just six years!

Suddenly I had three offices around the world and close to 100 employees. I was helping people, growing and earning millions at the same time. It was amazing.

The trouble was that I started to lose my way. I began forgetting that it was the system that brought my success, not my own golden touch. I wanted to go bigger, faster – I wanted to show up on the cover of Forbes.

So, I decided to try the impossible (because I could do anything). I decided to build a massive online education platform. An idea so explosive that it would rival Facebook in growth. Little did I know, I was now committing to learn some of the hardest lessons in my life.

The Fall To Near Bankruptcy

The minute I lost touch with the same things that had led to my success, I began making some devastating mistakes that I'll cover in detail later on in this book.

However, the biggest mistake I made was losing track of *who* an Entrepreneur really is. Instead, I fell in love with the *idea* of *what* an Entrepreneur is. It was during the next two years that I would see how impacted I was by society's views and definition of an Entrepreneur.

Long story short, I started investing money like an idiot.

I became oblivious to all the signs. I started ignoring everything going on around me. Instead, I began to blindly invest money in my business to chase a dream and a goal I knew nothing about. I was blinded by one desire: go big or go home.

Well, I literally had to go home. My parent's home.

Although it took me six years to create a $10 million a year company, it took less than two years to lose it all and fall *1.7 million in debt*. I owed money to everyone around me: credit cards, banks, family, friends, affiliates, vendors, lawyers – you name it. My own father mortgaged his entire home for me just to help me pay my ridiculous payroll.

Every time I think back to those days, I cringe. I had fallen so far that people around me were having to risk their lives just to save me. On the one hand, I was so grateful to have such amazing support. On the other hand, I was heartbroken, embarrassed, and tortured at what I had done.

The problem is that it didn't just impact my business. It destroyed everything. My health. My relationships. You name it, it was damaged.

I ended up in the hospital every three months with major internal bleeding from ulcers that would keep coming and going. I was constantly getting into fights with my friends, family, and everyone around me. All I could tell was that everything around me was falling apart and spiraling out of control.

And it was all because of me.

The Night I Learned The Most Important, Yet Simple Lesson...

Fast forward a few months and I nearly died – literally. I was on my way to attend a wedding in India and on a layover in Amsterdam. Somehow, I got bumped on my connecting flight to India and got stuck in Amsterdam for an entire night. Little did I know; it was a true blessing in disguise because that very night I started to fall very ill.

I spent the entire night curled in a corner of the room in torturous pain. So, rather than continuing to India, I decided to book the first flight in the morning back to the U.S. to go see my doctors.

As I woke up in the morning, I was in such bad shape that the only way I reached my gate at the airport was by setting 30 to 40 yard milestones. I would walk a bit and then allow myself to sit and rest, walk some more, sit and have some water. I did this all the way down what seemed like a never-ending airport terminal.

Finally, when I reached my gate, the agent at the door even stopped me and asked "*Are you okay sir?*" Startled by the fact that she could so easily tell something was wrong, I still lied and said "*yes, I just need to board and sleep.*"

Well, settling into my seat was the last thing I remember. Because the next thing I knew, I was waking up slowly and strapped to a stretcher. The plane was pulled over on the runway and had been stopped right before it took off. The mystery passenger next to me had noticed something wrong and waved down the flight attendant.

By the time they got me into an ambulance and got me to the hospital, I found out that I had bled out almost 40% of my blood.

Now, I was stranded in a random hospital in Amsterdam all alone. I was surrounded by strangers who spoke a different language and who had no idea what was wrong with me. Although the doctors managed to physically save my life that time, I knew that day that if I didn't make major changes I was going to eventually end up dead.

The ridiculous stress was reeking havoc on my body, especially on my digestive system that had been riddled with ulcers at this point. If I didn't make drastic changes and fast, I knew there would be a day where I wouldn't be able to reach the hospital fast enough.

That was when I looked at myself in the mirror and faced reality. What was I going to do? Cut and run or face the music? Was I going to take ownership over my life or would I let myself drown away in my "victim mentality" sorrows?

Thankfully, I decided to buckle down and fight back – there was no way I was going to go out this way.

I was released from the hospital within four days and under the escort of my parents, I safely flew back home. I don't think the plane had even landed in the U.S. before I decided to make some big changes.

- I shut down all my offices.
- I went from a team of nearly 100 employees to six.
- I shut down many of my products.
- I realigned my entire business.

Needless to say, the journey I embarked on was the hardest thing I have ever done in my life. Every day was a new day for me. Just battling the embarrassment alone was enough to keep me up every night. My health also continued to be challenging, I was still being hospitalized continuously as I fought to revive my life, but something was different, something still felt that I was moving in the right direction.

There was something inside me that just wouldn't give up.

On the night of my office closing, the night I would give my keys back to the landlord, I asked everyone to leave me alone in the office for a few hours. The truth is I had made a pact with myself that day. I had decided that I would NOT leave the office that night until I had figured out:

What the heck happened?
How did I go from the top to rock bottom so fast?
What mistakes had I made?

I sat in the empty office staring at a big white board in front of me. I started scribbling all over it. Any thought that came to me, I put it on the board. Before I knew it, the entire room looked like a scene from *A Beautiful Mind*. Actually, it looked kind of like I had *lost* my mind…

…but it was exactly the opposite. I was unlocking something huge.

After hours and hours of scribbling, I finally saw it – I discovered what happened.

It was so simple that it was almost cliché. And as much joy as it brought me, it also really ticked me off. I couldn't believe that I had let all my success go down the drain just because I had become so arrogant that I had abandoned the simplest system that had been working for me for years.

That was it! My own ego had betrayed me.

I had started trying things I knew nothing about. I had attempted things that had zero history – all while blatantly ignoring the very things that had worked for me for years!

I realized that of all the mistakes I had made, **99%** of them had *nothing* to do with the economy or money or customers or products.

The mistakes were mostly all about what was in my HEAD.

My thinking had become completely skewed. My belief of what and who an Entrepreneur is had become incredibly clouded. Well, it was time to fix all that – it was time to go back to the basics.

How I Got Back To The Top In 16 Months

With my head on straight, I went back to the system with a small, but deadly, team of six members. We were all in it for the same thing: to have a ferocious comeback. I now knew what mistakes I had made. I finally understood how to be an Entrepreneur.

I had it down to four stages, and it was time to climb back on each of them. In other words, it was time to get back to my core principles!

So, what happened?

In 16 months, I paid back *every single penny* of the $1.7 million I owed. I found my mojo again. I found my passion again. But most importantly, for the first time ever, I found my true purpose.

I made my comeback, all because I went back through the simple four stages of Entrepreneurial development.

Which brings me to the real purpose of this book.

Throughout this book, I will dissect my mistakes and my successes – all to help arrive at a simple code that helps you become a successful Entrepreneur.

These four stages are what you'll learn in the pages of this book.

You'll learn how to change your path of an employee mindset to an Entrepreneurial one. You'll learn how to create your own eSCAPE plan. Our journey together will take you through the following:

1. Self (Your Mind)
2. Catapult (Creating Momentum)
3. Authority (Building Leadership)
4. People (Your Environment)

Nail these stages and your eSCAPE plan will build itself.

However, before you go off trying to become an Entrepreneur, you need to know who an Entrepreneur really is because the definition you use is probably the one that society has taught you.

And it's not the right one...

CHAPTER 2:
WHAT IS AN ENTREPRENEUR?

When you type 'Entrepreneur' into Google, here's the definition you get...

"[1]a person who organizes and operates a business or businesses, [2] taking on greater than normal financial risks in order to do so."

This is where the problem starts. If I dissect this definition into two parts, I find it very misleading.

Part #1:
"[1]A person who organizes and operates a business or businesses..."

I disagree with this entire statement because I don't believe an Entrepreneur is defined by *what* they do. Instead, I believe an Entrepreneur is defined by *who* they are.

Entrepreneurship needs to be redefined to include the role an Entrepreneur plays, whether they run their own business or work for someone else. Entrepreneurship is so much more than simply running or launching a business.

Entrepreneurship Is A Mindset

Most would be surprised to hear that my opinion of Entrepreneurship actually has very little to do with running a business.

In today's world, someone can apply Entrepreneurship to pretty much every part of their life...

In the past, the "typical" Entrepreneur ran or started their own company. However, times have quickly changed with the latest technology companies out of Silicon Valley like...

- Google
- Yahoo!
- Amazon
- Apple
- Microsoft, Sony, 3M and other old-timers…

These companies have begun to function and operate completely differently. The term 'employee' is starting to disappear from these companies more and more every day.

Here's how…

See, an Entrepreneur is someone who claims a problem and decides to own the process of finding a solution to that problem. And that solution creates tremendous value in the lives of others.

An Entrepreneur has ownership, a team, freedom, and the responsibility of allocating their own resources.

By this definition, a scientist at the National Institute of Health is an Entrepreneur. A stay-at-home mother who starts a daycare service is an Entrepreneur. The lead developer who invents a new feature for their company, is also an Entrepreneur.

If anything, Entrepreneurship has become more about leadership today than any other time in history, but leadership is not only needed for *"running a business" – leadership is desperately needed in existing organizations too.*

Today, even the biggest companies are seeing their greatest successes thanks to a new concept called...

Because Intrapreneurship can be a difficult concept to understand at first, let's take a look at a few of the most famous products birthed from the Intrapreneurial spirit.

We can start with Facebook.

What do you do when you're surfing Facebook and see a post that you love? You click the like button! That famous button was developed during an Intrapreneurial event that Facebook regularly hosts for its employees called a hackathon.

Alright moving on, what about email?

On a daily basis, around 1.2 billion people send and receive emails using this particular service. Odds are that even you have an account with this particular service. So, which service am I talking about?

Gmail.

Gmail is another product of Intrapreneurship. This one product alone changed the entire future of Google. An "employee" actually came up with the idea during the "free time" that Google gives all of its team members.

Here's one more that happens to be one of my favorites…

Ken Kutaragi, a junior employee at Sony, became obsessed with tinkering with his daughter's Nintendo to make it better. He wanted to use his creativity to build a better product.

After years of having the freedom to play around with these ideas, Mr. Kutaragi helped Sony launch its now world-famous gaming system, the PlayStation.

This one Intrapreneur helped propel Sony to the top of a massively popular industry.

Yet another Intrapreneurial win.

In all these examples, all it took was one dedicated person owning a process. They…

- Discovered a problem or opportunity
- Created and innovated
- Led a team of people
- Solved a problem
- Created immense value

These individuals were not in business for themselves. They did not get an idea and run out to create a startup. Rather, they used the resources of their parent company to innovate. Even with these resources, they still took on all the stress, pressure, and responsibility of owning the entire journey.

It would be hard to argue that these people are not Entrepreneurs, and that's exactly where the term Intrapreneur comes from.

Looking past these conglomerates, my own company, Lurn, Inc., is a perfect example. Our company is full of Intrapreneurs, and their innovation has led to…

- A multi-million dollar joint venture with Robert Kiyosaki
- A product line that has done over $10 million in sales
- Reducing our support time to just over 2 hours
- The entire #LurnNation platform (Lurn.com)

Even though our amazing team members don't run their own companies, they do own their own departments. They're self-inspired, self-motivated, and self-managed.

So, there you have it. The first part of the traditional definition which said "[1]*a person who organizes and operates a business or businesses*" is no longer valid.

Now, for the second part...

Part #2:

"...taking on greater than normal financial risks in order to do so."

If possible, this is even more inaccurate than the first part of the definition. I disagree with the sentiment behind this statement, and I feel that it wrongly leads Entrepreneurs to create bad habits.

I know that it did for me.

The word 'risk' is a dangerous word that needs to be used carefully. It's true that Entrepreneurs go into the unknown, but that doesn't mean they're risk-takers in the way that we're taught to perceive the term.

Society has given us a very rogue, rebellious, and even reckless view of risk.

So, what is the impact this having?

This Misguided Definition Is Leading To More Failure...

The idea that Entrepreneurs are risk-takers is far from the truth. In fact, successful Entrepreneurs would never classify themselves as risk-takers. Instead, they'd argue that they're incredibly calculated.

By reinforcing the negative view of risk, we're drastically increasing the odds of failure through bad habits, thought patterns, and precedents.

When you go back to my story, the part where I fell $1.7 million in debt, the belief that I had to be a risk-taker was a big part of why I found myself trapped in the worst part of my life.

I was coasting along, running a company doing $10 million a year in revenue and growing year-over-year. Every project I touched was succeeding, so what was the risk? Where was the adrenaline rush? Was I playing it too safe?

I felt that I wasn't living up to what an Entrepreneur is supposed to be.

So, I wanted to make a splash. I wanted to build a billion dollar company. Millions weren't enough for me. However, at the rate I was growing it would take me more than a lifetime to get there. It was just too slow.

So, what did I do?

Because I wanted to be an Entrepreneur by society's definition, I decided to take a huge risk. I never even bothered to do a risk-reward analysis. Honestly, I didn't even know what that was.

I decided to throw it all in, even if it meant that I was going to stop doing everything that had been working all along.

The result?

I nearly destroyed my life, my health, my finances, my relationships—everything.

In hindsight, the Entrepreneur I am today would have never approached my idea the way I did back then.

The Word 'Risk' Is Misunderstood

Here's the thing about taking risks—society has taught us to see it as a bad thing.

The entire educational system is built to help protect us against any kind of risk. We're taught to go to school, go to college, get a degree, and find a nice, safe job. However, the truth is that times have changed—there's really no such thing as a "safe job" anymore.

The only surefire way to protect your job is to become a key innovator—someone who self-manages and leads efforts. That's exactly why Intrapreneurship is such a booming concept today.

Risk is now an innate part of life for everyone. However, **a successful Entrepreneur actually takes less risk in their life than the rest of the world.**

How can that be?

Successful Entrepreneurs are wise in the projects they attack, how they attack them, and how they plan their contingencies. Entrepreneurs who blindly approach ideas, throw in their life savings and take uncalculated risks are the reason why so many Entrepreneurs are known to fail.

How I Manage Risk

Fortunately for me, I learned a great lesson from nearly going bankrupt. Today, before I make a major decision or start a business, I conduct a full analysis. I look at all of the data available to me. I look at best-case scenarios, worst-case scenarios and everything in between.

I invest weeks, months, or even years preparing for a business before I ever consider launching it.

All of this comes back to habits, thinking patterns, and your mindset towards business. In other words, the S.C.A.P. formula. Mastering the four stages of S.C.A.P. helps assure that you, as an Entrepreneur, are always approaching a business with the right mindset.

Embrace The Unknown

The word 'risk' is misleading because it makes Entrepreneurs sound like gamblers. While many are gambling with their time and money, good Entrepreneurs are far from gamblers.

Instead, they're venturing into the unknown.

Having said that, the fact remains that most Entrepreneurs fail. Most Entrepreneurs have to shut their doors shortly after launching. For decades, we've been fed reasons as to why Entrepreneurs fail.

Personally, I don't agree with them, and I want to propose an entirely different way of thinking about Entrepreneurial failure.

CHAPTER 3:
WHY DO ENTREPRENEURS FAIL?

Let's get one thing straight—*ALL Entrepreneurs fail.*

Never live under the misconception that successful Entrepreneurs have never failed. In fact, they have probably failed more than anyone else. It's the successful Entrepreneurs we see at the top because they refuse to let their failures stop them.

The Entrepreneurs who succeed always understand that their failures are only temporary. They never quit because of failure; they learn from it, try over and over again, and keep at it until they prevail.

Still, the reality remains that the statistics aren't really in favor of Entrepreneurs...

Forbes reports that 80% of businesses fail within the first 18 months.

That's a 20% success rate beyond the first year and a half of a business, and the numbers get far worse when you get into three or five years past launch.

However, it's important not to let that number scare you because many Entrepreneurs are operating under the wrong definition of *who* an Entrepreneur is and *what* they do.

In this chapter, we're going to explore Entrepreneurial failure and the reasons behind it so that you can increase your chances of success.

Failing vs. Succeeding

Why do so many Entrepreneurs seem incapable of launching and running a successful long-term business?

I don't believe it's because they're incompetent.

In fact, the truth is quite the opposite. Most people who start their own businesses are very intelligent, daring, courageous, and ambitious.

So, what's really creating the failure?

For starters, Entrepreneurs are at a disadvantage from day one.

No matter who you ask, everyone has this perception that becoming an Entrepreneur is very risky. Thus, an Entrepreneur starts with the preconceived belief that they will most likely fail. Because of that perception, many Entrepreneurs are already prepared to fail. That, of course, is a big problem.

The second problem is that, from day one, Entrepreneurs are taught all the wrong reasons why so many Entrepreneurs fail. Some of the most common reasons cited by major publications as to why Entrepreneurs fail are:

- Not enough cash or cash flow.
- Product didn't have a market.
- Not a good business model.
- Issues with pricing and cost.
- Poor marketing.
- Ignoring customers.
- Bad timing.
- Lack of focus.
- Not pivoting in time.

I know that, when taken at face value, these reasons seem legitimate. A business is most certainly going to tank if it runs out of money, right? If a business doesn't market itself effectively, there's no way it can succeed, yes?

So when these issues pop up, people see them and put the blame on that reason alone. But me? I like to peel back one more layer.

I prefer to ask what caused these problems to come up in the first place.

Let's take your average Entrepreneur and call him Pete.

Pete can start any business.

He could open a small hardware store down the street. He could open a store that specializes in selling bicycles. He could open a home decoration specialty store. Heck, Pete could even start an *online* business selling custom-printed T-shirts.

His options are endless.

The bottom line is that Pete will conduct a full analysis of himself, of the market, and of his idea. Pete will then make a decision to start a business, whichever it is. Again, the focus here is that *Pete* had the idea, *Pete* did the analysis, and *Pete* made the decision to start that business.

Now let's assume the worst happens and Pete's business fails. He's closing it down. If you were to ask him what happened as he's shutting the door on his final day, he'd probably throw out several explanations like,

- Too much competition.
- Walmart undercut me.
- I didn't have enough money.
- It's too tough for small businesses.
- There is not enough support out there.
- I had bad employees.
- This isn't the right area for this kind of business.

On the surface, Pete might even appear to be right. I mean, we can all sympathize with the idea of an evil corporation coming into a small town and assassinating all the small businesses. We can even have great compassion and empathy for that.

However, I believe Pete's blame would be misplaced.

All these reasons above are *external* factors. By using these as excuses, Pete is taking absolutely no responsibility for his failure. He's missing a couple of important questions.

- What caused these problems to begin with?
- What allowed them to keep happening?

I say this because no matter what small town you visit, you'll find small businesses that are thriving despite being right down the street from a company like Walmart. So, what do these businesses know that Pete doesn't?

The problem is that we've been taught for decades to immediately go into self-preservation mode when bad things happen. We quickly look to console ourselves. We don't want to feel the pain of defeat, so we create a scenario that justifies our actions and excuses our shortcomings.

While this may help you feel better, it's robbing you of the gift of learning from your experience. By not owning up to our own role in failure, we never get the chance to improve and grow.

Our friend Pete has the classic victim mentality that allows the cycle of failure to continue. It's everyone else's fault, not his. He truly believes that all of these external factors led to his downfall, which allows him to protect himself from the embarrassment and disappointment of having failed.

Think about it. When is the last time you heard someone say,

- I failed because I didn't work hard enough.
- I failed because I didn't learn fast enough.
- I failed because I didn't really have a purpose or a why.
- I failed because I didn't pivot or make the right decisions at the right times.

Notice the number of times the word 'I' came up in those statements. It's not easy to take that ownership because it makes one take full responsibility and live up to their mistakes. Although it may not be easy, taking full ownership is the only way to grow.

Why Entrepreneurs Really Fail

So if Pete didn't fail because of all the external factors, why did he fail?

You fail because of what you do or don't do, not what is done or not done to you.

Even at my lowest point, when I was *$1.7 million* in debt, I never looked outside of myself to determine why I had failed. I only looked at myself to see what I did or didn't do.

I spent hours at the whiteboard in my empty office. I said to myself, "*I'm going to lock myself in this room and not leave until I figure out what the heck went wrong; Just exactly why I failed?*"

I was determined to dive deep into myself to figure out what I had done or not done to create the current circumstance I was in.

I truly believe that no one talks about the real reasons Entrepreneurs fail because no one wants to face them. No one wants to admit that it mostly comes down to a lack of accountability and responsibility.

We learn this way of thinking from a young age.

Since we were children, our environment has mostly taught us to always self-preserve.

Think about when you and another kid got in trouble for fighting at school. If you stood up and accepted the blame, you'd get yelled at by the teacher. So what do you do instead? Find a way to shift the blame.

Failed a test? The teacher didn't cover the topics well enough in class.

Got into a fight? The other kid started it.

Got in trouble? You didn't do anything!

This mentality starts in our childhood and continues into our adulthood.

For example, just think for a second, if you were to march into your boss's office and take full blame for a major loss that just happened, there is a good chance that you may get fired. So, instead, over years, you've learned ways to avoid taking responsibility and live to work another day.

It's just survival.

The only problem is that in the world of Entrepreneurship, the self-preservation tactics that you've learned over the years will actually lead to your demise instead of your survival.

Patrick's Story

Take Patrick, an Entrepreneur I met a year ago.

He worked hard and built an online business up to $2 million a year in revenue. Everything was going great for him. That is, until he faced his first challenge. There was a new competitor in the market and Patrick's business had quickly started to decline.

However, Patrick never worried. The product that Patrick sold was a very unique product that he had created himself. He was even in the process of getting a patent for it. As far as Patrick knew, he was set for life. He would just continue to expand the sales of his new creation.

However, his competitor had other plans. The competition came in with a similar product that had better features and sold at a lower price. In Patrick's mind, his competitor cheated him and violated his pending patent. Although he was probably right, that didn't stop the inevitable from happening. Patrick spent months and tens of thousands of dollars trying to legally fight his competitor, but his pockets weren't deep enough to survive.

When Patrick walked away and closed his doors, his exact words to me were, "Because the government wouldn't protect me, my business is gone. I lost everything."

Now, you might think that sounds reasonable. Even I agree that what happened to Patrick was horrible. His rights were violated and someone stole from him. I truly have a lot of sympathy for Patrick, but at the same time, I'm ready to ask the tough questions.

For starters, no business dies overnight. Most take months, if not longer, to die. Patrick's business was no different. I asked Patrick when his competitor had come into the market with their product. Patrick's answer left me shocked. He told me that the competitor had come into the market over a year and a half ago.

A year and a half!

The entire time he was talking to me, all I could think about was his missed opportunities. He had a year and a half to pivot. He had a year and a half to redo his product or come up with another product. He had a year and half to launch a different division. He had a year and a half to go into a new market.

He did not fail because this competitor came in and stole his product. Patrick failed because he was not ready and willing to do the things we're going to talk about in this book.

The bottom line is — **we fail because of how we make decisions.** We fail because of the internal programming we've been building for decades.

Although you had no control over the programming and messages you received when you were younger, you don't have to blindly accept that programming. You can reprogram yourself, and that's why I'm bringing eSCAPE into the World.

It's the formula that helps you unwind some of the bad programming.

Mastering eSCAPE

Success or failure. Either way, it's all about *you*. It's about how you remove the old programming and replace it with something that will propel you forward rather than hold you back.

Nearly every business that fails does so because the Entrepreneur didn't have the knowledge or the confidence they needed to overcome the challenges that came their way.

However, these are all things that can be changed. They're skills that you can learn.

This is where the S.C.A.P. formula comes in.

We're just getting the engines revved up. Let's keep attacking some of the tough questions, and then we'll move into the key characteristics of becoming a powerful Entrepreneur.

The next question I want to explore is one that I hear all the time...

"Anik, can *anyone* become an Entrepreneur?"

My answer to this question may surprise you.

CHAPTER 4:
CAN ANYONE BE AN ENTREPRENEUR?

It turns out that a lot of people want to be Entrepreneurs.

According to the Organization for Economic Co-operation and Development, **69%** of men and **58%** of women say they want to become an Entrepreneur. Not only that, but Entrepreneurial aspirations appear to be trickling down to younger generations as well. Forbes reports that **62%** of Millennials want to start their own business.

Despite the desire that so many people have to run their own business, the number of actual Entrepreneurs is surprisingly low. The Global Entrepreneurship Monitor reported in 2015 that just under **14%** of Americans were starting or running a new business.

But here's the thing about that 14%…

It only refers to the traditional concept of the Entrepreneur, someone who starts their own company. However, as we discussed earlier, there are two types of Entrepreneurs. One of them, the Intrapreneur, still works for someone else.

So, Can Anyone Be A Successful Entrepreneur?

The answer to this question is more complicated than a simple yes or no. Theoretically, yes, anyone can become an Entrepreneur. However, you're going to have to work much harder to succeed if you aren't naturally inclined toward the Entrepreneurial lifestyle.

Look at it this way.

I do very well as an Entrepreneur, but could I become a physicist? If I applied myself, I'm sure I could dogfight my way into becoming a physicist even though I'd be miserable in that field.

Now, let's look at my friend Sally who actually is a physicist. She loves it. Sally is naturally inclined toward physics because her brain is wired to be able to see the math in the theories. Mine? Not so much. So, who will have an easier and more fun time becoming a physicist?

But on the flip side, even though she's highly intelligent and could succeed as an Entrepreneur, Sally's personality isn't geared toward an Entrepreneurial lifestyle in the way that mine is.

The Real Question You Should Be Asking

Actually, I believe that everyone is asking the wrong question when they ask, "Can I become an Entrepreneur?" The question they should be asking is, "Is it *worth it* for me to become an Entrepreneur?"

As a part of this book, I'm going to introduce a rating score called your **eSCORE**. The purpose of this score is to help you understand how likely you are to naturally succeed as an Entrepreneur.

To get your eSCORE, take our free quiz at: www.Lurn.com/quiz.

In short, the higher your eSCORE is, the higher your chances are of succeeding as an Entrepreneur. The lower your eSCORE is, the harder you'll have to work to raise your odds of succeeding. The system will also analyze you on each of the elements we're about to discuss: S.C.A.P. Once you've taken the quiz, the results page will explain in more detail how to analyze your results.

Although the purpose of this quiz is to help you get a start and an initial understanding of whether or not you're equipped to begin the Entrepreneurial journey, it's important to remember that the results are not set in stone. After reading this book and applying its teachings, you can always come back and take the quiz again. You can watch your eSCORE grow, but you can also monitor your weaknesses so that you can focus your training and growth in the areas that need it the most.

Once you've taken the test, you'll be equipped with the necessary information to really determine whether or not it's worth it to you to begin this journey.

I have a very close friend who's probably at least twice as smart as me. The guy can figure out anything and everything that you ask him. Because of that, he has an amazing job that is incredibly competitive. He's conquered "the system" and naturally risen to the top.

However, as they say – the grass is always greener on the other side.

While he was busy getting his master's degree and working up the corporate ladder, he was watching me take the Entrepreneurial path. He saw me travel the World, drive my beautiful cars, and win awards. Naturally, he started asking me for my help because suddenly, he also wanted to become an Entrepreneur.

So, I did what any good friend would do and offered him a helping hand.

Months would go by and he'd fizzle out. Months later, he'd reawaken and come after me again. However, he'd get a deeper look into my life with each burst. More and more, he'd see the less glamorous side of my life. He'd see the decisions I made on a daily basis, the stress, and the sacrifices.

Fast forward to today and he's no longer interested in becoming an Entrepreneur. So, what happened? Why couldn't this incredibly successful man make it as an Entrepreneur?

Simple.

One day, he came to me and said, "You know what? I don't think I want to do this. I can't do the things you do. I don't want to be an Entrepreneur." He just couldn't, or didn't want to, face the things that I face on a daily basis.

He went on to get promoted at work, makes great money, and is now living the life of an Intrapreneur. He's happy. He's fulfilled. He's growing.

And guess what?

There's nothing wrong with that at all.

In the end, whether you become an Entrepreneur, Intrapreneur, or employee is truly a *personal decision*. No one can make that choice for you.

Remember, I started out going to school for medicine. I wanted to become a doctor. If I had stayed there, could I have become a doctor? I'm sure I could have. It would have been a lot of hard work, especially for me, but I'm confident in myself – I'm capable and I'm hard-working.

See, anatomy, biology, and chemistry are not subjects that come naturally to me. Today, I cringe at even the sound of knuckles cracking. Imagine how hard it would have been for me to hold a scalpel and help in a surgery!

But that's the thing - who wants a life where they are constantly having to brute force their way through something just to do it? That's exactly why I left that path. My desire to become a doctor was nowhere near great enough for what I would have had to put in to succeed.

So I chose to become an Entrepreneur, a career that I had no mentorship in, knew nothing about, and that everyone told me was risky.

However, I had exactly what I needed the most for an Entrepreneurial career: desire and passion.

So, What About You?

If you want to become an Entrepreneur, you'll have to answer some tough questions about yourself, like...

- Is being an Entrepreneur a natural fit for you?
- How hard will you have to work to succeed?
- Is it worth the effort?
- Is it something you want badly enough?

Again, to get an idea of what your path to becoming an Entrepreneur is going to look like, go to www.Lurn.com/quiz to take the eSCORE quiz.

No matter what your eSCORE is, I do believe that anyone can become a successful Entrepreneur because we're all born as Entrepreneurs. The process of growing up is what changes things.

In the next chapter, I'll explain my theory.

CHAPTER 5:
BORN ENTREPRENEURS,
WHAT HAPPENED?

Sarah is a diligent employee.

She works hard and rarely calls in sick. Even when she does, she feels guilty. Despite being a great employee, she recently turned 40 years old and still hasn't earned the promotion to management that she's been working toward all these years.

To make her goal happen, what do you think she should do? Work harder? Work longer hours? Well, 9 out of 10 times, Sarah's going to do just that.

Sound familiar?

This could be *anyone's* story. The customer service rep at your cell phone company, the bank teller at your local branch, or the cashier at your local grocery store. Heck, there's even a good chance that you're in this exact same position.

Why? Because we've all been raised to become employees.

We've all been taught to work as hard as needed until others are impressed and grant us our wishes.

Your parents, your siblings, your friends, you and even me. The truth is that we've all been brainwashed to think and act like employees. It's just how our educational system is designed.

Babson College published an interesting report with a breakdown of small business ownership:

- 51% of small business owners are over the age of 50.
- 33% of small business owners are ages 35-49.
- 16% of small business owners are under the age of 35.

If you graphed this data, you could see the impact of being in our educational system for two decades. The minute most people graduate or leave school, the natural next step is to go get a job. As they get older, many see the fault in their line of thinking.

More and more people start becoming Entrepreneurs as they get older. It takes years and years, but many do see the reality of how what we're taught and what we need is so different.

So indulge me for a minute because I've got a bit of a crazy theory.

My theory is that we're actually all born Entrepreneurs at heart, but the system beats it out of us. Let me explain…

Everyone Is Born An Entrepreneur

Babies are incredible learners. Have you ever watched a toddler? Their ability to learn and adapt to new environments is amazing. Their ability to build creative solutions is equally as impressive.

Just think about the first year of life. Babies learn to sit up, eat, crawl, walk, run, talk, build with blocks and so much more. The best part is that they fail repeatedly during this time, but it never seems to hold them back.

For example, imagine a child trying to walk. They fall over and over and over, yet it never phases them. They don't stop trying until they're finally walking. Basically, all they know is that they can do it. They look around and see everyone else around them walking, so they keep trying until they succeed. They have no other outcome in their mind.

Just consider it for a moment - this very way of *thinking* and *being* is incredibly Entrepreneurial in its own right. They see that their method of movement, crawling, is slower than everyone else's. So, they take ownership of solving their problem no matter how many times they fail.

The problem is that this Entrepreneurial spirit begins to crumble, piece by piece, once we start being told what to do by those around us. The first time we hear the word 'no' or the first time we're stopped from exploring our curiosity, it begins a process that lasts for decades.

We're surrounded by authoritative figures who start to shape what we believe we can and cannot do.

What Do You Want To Be When You Grow Up?

When my nephew was just three years old, he told me he wanted to be the sidekick to Iron Man, a.k.a War Machine, when he grew up. I was tickled by the confidence he had in his voice, so I decided to do a quick experiment.

I wanted to see how he'd react if I told him he couldn't be War Machine. I wanted to see what his reaction would be to being told something was impossible. So I told him that War Machine wasn't real and that it was just a movie character.

Wow, did I regret that experiment quickly.

My nephew immediately got angry, very angry. He acted absolutely shocked, annoyed and appalled. He actually looked at me like I was the crazy one. He even went out of his way to tell me that I didn't know what I was talking about.

I couldn't help but chuckle and give him a high five. He may have only been three years old, but no one was going to tell him what he could or could not do. I loved it. The truth is that he's not alone. Actually, most children would react the same way because children are born Entrepreneurs.

They make bold statements. They take on courageous challenges, and they attempt everything that seems impossible. Unfortunately, most only hold on to the Entrepreneurial spirit for so many years before it burns out.

As they grow older, more and more people in society start to shape their beliefs based on what others tell them is impossible.

As we get older and progress through grade school, life becomes defined by the expectations set by other people. Our parents begin to make decisions for us. They decide what after-school activities we enroll in, what time we sleep, what food we eat and so much more. When we're not with our parents, we have teachers and coaches who make a living telling us what to do.

It isn't long before we start prioritizing pleasing others over our own wishes and dreams. We start valuing ourselves by the praise we receive from others. Essentially, we focus on their goals for us, not our own.

It actually gets worse from there.

As we go through high school, we start studying for exams and trying to perfect our grades. Why? Well, because we need to get into college. Everything about us will be summarized on a few pages and suddenly strangers we've never met will read these few pages to determine whether we're worthy enough to gain admission to their university.

So, now we're working years and years to impress someone we'll never even meet!

Then we actually make it into college and right away begin building a resume so that we can impress a recruiter someday in hopes of getting a job.

Again, we're working hard to impress others, studying and doing the things that they deem important.

Let's assume that all goes well and we finally get a job. Our days of needing to impress other people are finished, right? Not even close. We've actually placed ourselves into this cycle for the rest of our lives.

We'll get up every morning and go to sleep every night working to impress our boss, praying for a promotion, and hoping to get wealthy through our salary raises.

The worst part is that through all of these experiences, never once are we learning to think about our own dreams or prioritize our own wishes. It's literally not in our upbringing or in our educational system.

The Problem Is Self-Accountability

The result of living our entire upbringing trying to impress others is that we never learn what it means to be accountable and responsible to ourselves. What I find is that many Entrepreneurs struggle with discipline and responsibility from day one.

Why?

Because they don't have a boss anymore.

They have no one they fear. They have no one who could fire them. Don't want to wake up? No problem. Just hit the snooze button. In a job, you'd be tripping over your pants to get to work on time because if you didn't - well, you know what would happen.

Being able to hit the snooze button 10 times may sound like a great thing, but it actually symbolizes great disaster.

The thing is that it's not really your fault.

If a baseball player can't throw a football, no one will blame him. After all, he was never taught that skill. He was taught to throw a baseball. So it really comes back to the system that we're in.

Now, I don't want to sound like I'm completely bashing the system or saying that it doesn't do anyone any good. Obviously the system has survived for centuries because it actually works for a number of people. In fact, many people have become extremely wealthy from it. However, times have changed, and we risk being left behind if we don't start questioning the system.

All in all, from the time we enter the educational system, we are taught what I call the "employee mentality." This is a thinking pattern that helps you excel as an employee, but can directly destroy your attempt to become an Entrepreneur.

The greatest difference between an employee and an Entrepreneur is where they find their strength, courage, and motivation. Compared to an employee, an Entrepreneur always finds their purpose and inspiration inside themselves, not from someone else.

Not long ago, I was having a conversation with someone and we were talking about dreams, goals, and success. After about five minutes of conversation, my counterpart clearly became frustrated and blurted out, "What's the point of dreaming big when you're never going to be able to reach that dream?"

I was speechless.

I could tell that very minute that this person was not alone. It broke my heart to think that there are literally billions of people walking around this world every day with this core belief. They don't even bother to dream because they realize their entire lives are already committed to someone else's dreams.

Let me say it now, and I'll say it over and over again: Today, more than ever, **you** have control over your own dreams. It's easier today to live your life purely for your own dream than ever before.

And, remember – you do not have to start your own business to fight for your own dreams, Intrapreneurs all over the World are doing it daily within the safe environment of a big organization. The key is to find autonomy and control over what you're doing and why you're doing it.

So, take a moment right now and ask yourself, are you currently waiting to make your dream real because you're too busy making ends meet? Who are you more dedicated to impressing, yourself or someone else?

Be honest.

The reason so few Entrepreneurs succeed is because many never get out of this trap. Many never master the self-accountability that's necessary to succeed. So, how do the others do it? Well, they either had a unique upbringing to boost an independent mindset or they've invested a lot of time and money in the right education and training.

For me, it was reading the right books and finding the right mentors. Fortunately, I found these resources early enough and was able to put the rest together. Today, my goal for you is that you use this book to catch all the things that may be holding you back.

My hope is that you'll be able to find all traces of the employee mentality that have been placed inside of you. Given the resources you're about to find, hopefully you can break free from all of these constraints.

The first step in doing this is to understand the **core differences** between the employee and Entrepreneur mentality.

In the next chapter, that's exactly what we're going to discuss....

CHAPTER 6:
THE CORE DIFFERENCES BETWEEN
AN EMPLOYEE AND AN ENTREPRENEUR

The most important thing to take away from what we've discussed so far is...

An Entrepreneur is *who* we are, not *what* we are.

This means it all comes back to us and how we think about ourselves. It's our mindset that matters, and there are five core differences between the way Entrepreneurs think and the way those with an employee mindset think.

These five differences truly set Entrepreneurs apart:

1. Time
2. Money
3. Problems
4. Dreams
5. Struggle

Let's dive into the details...

Time

Time is limited. We only have **24 hours** in a day—no more, no less. There's nothing we can do to change that.

Both employees and Entrepreneurs share one thing in common regarding how they perceive time: they both look at time as a scarce commodity. Beyond that, their approach to and beliefs about time are completely different.

For employees, time is divided into two distinct areas—*their* time (work) and *my* time (personal).

When an employee is at work, it's *their* time. That's the time they devote to their employer so they can get a paycheck. When they leave work, they consider it *my* time. They go home, lie on the sofa and watch TV or go to the local happy hour to hang out with their friends. Alright, that may sound harsh but what I mean is that typically, an employee mindset will choose to do whatever makes them happy or allows them to decompresses from a hard day of working for the "man."

In short, an employee will take their *my time* and aim to maximize their enjoyment. Unfortunately, that time rarely involves working on something for their own dreams.

And that's it.

People with the employee mindset generally trade time for either money or enjoyment, and they often do this for their entire life.

How Entrepreneurs View Time

Entrepreneurs have a very different idea of how to use their time. To them, time holds immense value and should be *invested*.

It comes back to that old saying, *time is money*. To an Entrepreneur, time is the most valuable asset they have, not money. They understand the direct correlation between how they invest their time and the likelihood of achieving their dreams.

Did you know that Entrepreneurs actually work more hours than employed people? Gallup Poll News reports that 49% of self-employed people work more than 44 hours a week, compared to only 39% of employed people.

Despite working more, The New York Times conducted a study that found that business owners are happier and feel more fulfilled than the average employee. So Entrepreneurs are failing more often and working more hours, but they're also happier and more fulfilled.

Pretty interesting, right?

I always find this data funny because most people think that becoming an Entrepreneur is all about achieving *the freedom to do whatever you want.* How does that work if you're actually working more than someone who's employed?

It's simple.

True Entrepreneurs love what they do so much that they choose to do work in their free time.

When I was in college, I was fully invested in my business and personal growth. I worked crazier hours during these years than I ever have.

- I was a full-time student.
- I was taking extra classes to get ahead.
- I was a part-time financial planner.
- I had my own online business.
- I was enrolled in personal development courses.

I was doing all of this at the same time. Here's what my typical day was like:

- Go to classes all day and finish around 4:00 or 5:00 p.m.
- Meet with financial planning clients until 8:00 or 9:00 p.m.
- Head home and finish my school work.
- Stay up until 2:00 or 3:00 a.m. to work on my online business.
- Sleep for four or five hours.
- Repeat.

I never had time for college football games, frat parties, or weekends out at the bar with my friends. In fact, it was rare to see me out at all. Although I never had any free time in my life for social things, I actually had the most freedom out of all my friends after we graduated!

So, what was the result of my wise time investment?

I grew, my business grew, and I earned incredible money. I never even had to get a job because I was already earning over $500,000 per year by the time I graduated. I had full freedom to do exactly what I wanted to do.

Imagine that.

My peers were jumping for joy at $50,000 offers and here I was making 10 times more than that. I guess skipping a few football and basketball games paid off.

So, what's the takeaway?

Time is an opportunity. Use it wisely. Instead of turning on the TV when you get home from work or after you've put the kids to bed, consider how else you can use that time.

How can you invest that time into bettering yourself or getting closer to making your dreams come true?

Money

We all need to earn a living. We need to pay for the roof over our heads and the food on the table. Everyone needs money, and almost everyone wishes that they had more of it.

In many ways, money is the axis around which all of our lives spin.

However, money is one area where employees and Entrepreneurs think very differently.

How Employees View Money

Employees see money as a tool—*as a means to buy things needed for survival.*

They spend eight hours at work every day in a trade for money. Once they get that paycheck, they use it to pay their bills and meet other financial responsibilities. They then take the rest of that paycheck and head to a store to go shopping. Or many take a chunk and start saving it for the future so they can retire but still afford to live.

Money is nothing more than a trading unit for someone stuck in the employee mindset—a finite quantity much like time. Employees earn it, spend it, or save it to eventually spend it. However, the hard truth is that most employees never manage to save much money, at least not enough to get out of the rat race.

How Entrepreneurs View Money

Entrepreneurs see money as a vehicle, *a means to an end.* To them it's a living, breathing organism that should be invested to foster growth.

Notice that word again—INVESTED.

To the Entrepreneur, money doesn't have a finite value. Instead, it can be put to work to make even more money. Entrepreneurs see a future in which they can make money work for them instead of spending their lives working for money.

However, getting money to work for you is not instant gratification. It takes years of patience and shrewd investment. This is exactly why most people with an employee mindset struggle with money. They get money and use it to satisfy their desire for instant gratification.

Because of this mindset, investing in something like a business course that costs $2,000 is difficult for many people. They'll sit and sweat over the decision for hours, debating, aching and finding themselves unable to pull the trigger. The list of reasons they create as to why they shouldn't spend that money grows too long for them to justify investing in themselves.

However, that same person won't hesitate even a moment to run to a local store and throw down $1,000 on a new TV or $50,000 for a new car. Again, for those stuck in the employee mindset, many times, it's mostly about the desire for immediate satisfaction.

So, what would an Entrepreneur do with that same $50,000?

An Entrepreneur would take their $50,000, downgrade to a $30,000 car and save $20,000 to invest in themselves or their business.

Entrepreneurs are the first to invest in anything to do with their business—education, equipment, resources or mentoring. Most will readily make sacrifices in their personal life to invest in themselves or their business because they have the ability to look and think ahead.

So again, money is a tool for both employees and Entrepreneurs. Employees just typically use it for more immediate satisfaction, while Entrepreneurs use it to invest for the future.

Problems

Problems are a fact of life—I think everyone can agree on that.

We face problems every single day of our lives. They can be small problems, such as locking our keys in the car, or they can be large problems like losing a job.

Believe it or not, it's how we *view* problems that makes the deepest impact on our lives. And employees see problems *very* differently than Entrepreneurs do.

How Employees View Problems

To employees, problems are bad. Just flat out bad. They're troublesome, annoying, unnecessary, and downright evil. In fact, they're to be avoided at all costs. When problems can't be avoided, people in the employee mindset immediately pass them off to someone else.

To an employee, problems represent obstacles that get in the way of enjoying their life.

How Entrepreneurs View Problems

Entrepreneurs have a much different reaction to problems.

Entrepreneurs see problems as *opportunities*—to grow, to learn, and to do better than before.

They take immediate ownership over them, even solving a problem that's not theirs just so they can feel the satisfaction of owning the process and finding a solution.

The reason why an Entrepreneur embraces problems so quickly is because they view problems as an obstacle between them and their ultimate dream. It's not about short-term happiness, which is why they're not phased by the problem. What really concerns them is their long-term goal, so they will do anything they can to clear the way.

Entrepreneurs quickly jump into "solve mode." They immediately break problems down into manageable pieces, and they're very strategic and execution-oriented.

In fact, most great Entrepreneurs discover some of their great creations inside of a major problem. If you think about the business ventures or inventions that have changed the course of mankind, they were all the result of an Entrepreneur owning and solving a problem.

Take something as simple as the Q-tip. While the Q-tip may seem trivial, this invention was massive. Just try to imagine your bathroom without Q-tips. This entire invention came about because Leo Gerstenzang watched his wife trying to stick a cotton swab on the end of a toothpick. Once he saw the problem, he went to work to create a solution.

An employee would throw the toothpick away in frustration. An Entrepreneur, however, took the problem, owned it, and thus the Q-tip was born.

66

I would wager that nearly everyone dreams about their future from a very early age. As we get older, dreams become less and less important to the majority of the world.

Why?

Well, look at the data...

An astounding 94% of people never achieve their childhood dreams. Not only that, but we can't even handle our smaller goals. Studies show that 92% of people don't even make their New Year's resolutions stick!

There's a lot of people roaming the streets today who are capable of having big dreams, but they don't even try to achieve them because they think the odds against them are stacked too high.

How Employees View Dreams

The employee mindset is, *I'll think about what my dream is when I have more money or when I get a promotion.* They're literally waiting for external factors to give them permission to think about their own dreams.

To the employee, dreams might, just maybe, happen someday later on if they wait long enough. They believe that dreams are for the privileged few. Their dreams are something they can have later in their life if things happen to go in their favor.

The thing is, most people don't actually believe they'll reach that level of success. For this reason, most people believe they won't ever reach their dreams. Instead, they give in and just go through life *as it is.*

How Entrepreneurs View Dreams

To an Entrepreneur, there is no life without dreams. They believe that achieving their dream is an innate right.

Entrepreneurs will stop at nothing to make their dreams come true. In fact, they live in their dream all the time. They're dreaming day and night about what they want to accomplish, and some even take it too far and start living in their own fantasies!

See, there's no point to life for an Entrepreneur if they can't chase their dreams.

The "Why"

It all has to do with your "why."

Why are you working and earning money? *Why* are you getting out of bed every day? Is it just to pay the bills, or do you want to do something greater?

An employee's "why" is very limited. For them it's about paying the bills. They're only thinking ahead to the next paycheck. That's their "why."

On the other hand, the Entrepreneur's "why" is to create, change, impact and influence—to do something so big that it changes the world.

For Entrepreneurs, it's bigger than just themselves.

Struggle

Just as it is full of problems, life is also full of struggle.

It's a fact of life, so why not embrace it?

After all, *nothing that is worth having in life comes easily.* Again, employees and Entrepreneurs view struggle very differently.

How Employees View Struggle
Employee + no struggle = happy

As with problems, employees view struggle as a bad thing. Those with the employee mindset believe that it's better to take the easiest possible path and avoid struggle at all costs.

How Entrepreneurs View Struggle
Entrepreneur + struggle = progress

Entrepreneurs know that struggle only makes them stronger.

They thrive when faced with struggle.

Struggle Is Like Weight-Lifting

To an Entrepreneur, struggle represents opportunity. The more an Entrepreneur struggles, the more it hurts, the closer they are to making a breakthrough.

But most employees highly prefer the easy way out.

Imagine you're at a gym and a trainer tells you to grab the 20-pound dumbbell and do 10 reps. As soon you start, you can feel the burn. You know just how much it's going to hurt. About five reps in, it's really hard.

An employee would put the 20-pound dumbbell down, pick up the 1-pound dumbbell and finish the 10 reps.

But by taking the path of least resistance, they're only cheating themselves, They'll never get any stronger since they aren't willing to push through the exercise when it gets difficult.

An Entrepreneur, however, will pick up the 20-pound dumbbell and do as many reps as they can. If they don't make 10 reps, they won't give up. They'll keep pushing harder and harder. They'll push until their arm literally collapses, but they'll never pick up the 1-pound dumbbell.

They understand that if they can't do 10 reps that day, they just need to keep trying over and over. They know that, before long, 10 reps will become easy.

The truth is that it does get easier, but that's not even the crazy part.

The crazy part is that the very day that the Entrepreneur gets their 10 reps in, they won't take a minute to celebrate. They'll reach for the 30-pound dumbbell to start the process all over again.

The bottom line is that an Entrepreneur understands that it's only through struggle that one can grow. It's when there's no struggle that there's a problem.

It's All About Changing Your Perspective

As we go through the S.C.A.P. process and create your eSCAPE plan, we'll work within these five core areas. Going through S.C.A.P. will allow you to fine tune your skills and abilities so that you can gain a new perspective on these five core disciplines.

First, you'll find out whether you think like an employee or an Entrepreneur. Then you'll learn exactly what you need to do to continue your growth in each specific area.

In fact, the S.C.A.P. system and your mastery of it will determine how likely you are to succeed as an Entrepreneur.

CHAPTER 7:
S.C.A.P. INTRODUCED

Everyone who considers becoming an Entrepreneur asks the same types of questions. Questions like,

- Do I have the money?
- Do I have a good idea?
- Can I handle the risk?
- Will I succeed?

Unfortunately, these aren't the questions that will make the deepest impact on your chances of success.

You see, using metrics that most never bother to think about, there's actually a way for us to put a number, *a score*, on your personal probability of succeeding as an Entrepreneur.

I call it your *eSCORE*, and we're going to dive deeper into that in this chapter.

The entire purpose of studying S.C.A.P. is so that you can focus on increasing your *eSCORE*, and the way you do that is by developing your own *eSCAPE plan*. Your plan is going to look different than everyone else's. It'll be completely unique to your own strengths, weaknesses, and surroundings.

My goal is to empower you with the information in this book so that you can create a roadmap tailored to your own life experience, a plan specific to you.

The eSCAPE Plan

The eSCAPE plan isn't about determining where you're going—I'm already assuming that you're reading this book because you aspire to become an Entrepreneur.

The eSCAPE plan is really about determining the areas that you need to strengthen to experience Entrepreneurial success. So, the plan starts with a detailed analysis on each of the four stages below:

1. Self
2. Catapult
3. Authority
4. People

However, we don't stop at the four stages. From there, we get even more detailed.

Each of these four stages is broken down further into five elements. So within each of the four stages, I'm going to cover five key lessons and traits that help determine what your score is in that particular area.

Think of these five lessons as a way of breaking down that specific stage into manageable pieces. Each lesson is mapped out to help you understand where you are today and what you need to focus on for tomorrow.

But here's the best part...

You don't need to master all five lessons in each of the four stages. As a matter of fact, I highly doubt that there's a single Entrepreneur on the face of this planet, including myself, that has mastered all of them.

The underlying theme is that the more you master, the better off you are.

The Four Stages—S.C.A.P.

Each of the four stages of S.C.A.P. (going from employee to Entrepreneur) are pieces to the overall puzzle of success. Let's take a closer look at each of them.

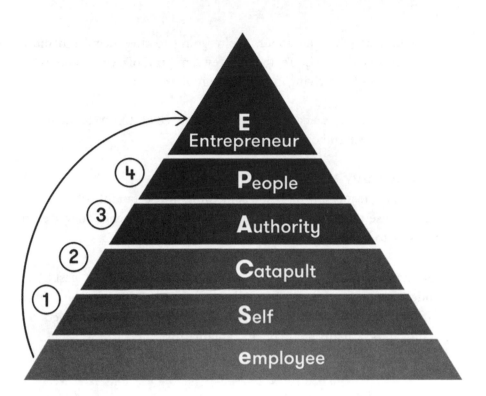

Stage #1: Self

This stage is about what's going on inside your mind, and it's the first area we must address. If your mindset, mentality, paradigms, and thought patterns are not aligned with those of an Entrepreneur, nothing else is going to matter.

In this stage, we'll go over the key changes in *thinking* that you need to succeed as an Entrepreneur.

Stage #2: Catapult

There are certain characteristics that help us to get started and create momentum.

It's like trying to push a car that's stalled.

Initially, it will take a lot of effort from several people to get the car going. However, once the car starts rolling, just one person could coast along with one hand on the car to keep it going.

That's what catapult is all about. We're going to dive deep into those initial moments that require the greatest amount of work, and we'll discuss strategies for thriving in that environment.

Creating momentum is a core function that a successful Entrepreneur will need to repeat over and over in their lifetime.

Stage #3: Authority

Authority and leadership are not something we're taught when we're young. Because of the way the system is set up, most people never even get a chance to learn these skills.

Just think about your years in school. Each class would have at least 25 to 30 students in it, but how many students got to be a class leader? Only one. If you played football growing up, you probably had 60 players on the team, but how many got to be the captain? Just one.

The odds of mastering leadership have been against us from the beginning, but it's not too late.

Together, we can change this.

Stage #4: People

Last, but certainly not least, we have people.

No matter how confident you are in your abilities, nobody can become a successful Entrepreneur alone. We need a network of the right people around us to help us achieve our dreams. In addition to having the right people, we need the right energy, attitude, and environment.

Controlling your environment, and the people in it, can be one of the most difficult elements of becoming a successful Entrepreneur. It's certainly one of the areas that I struggled with the most.

However, the good news is I've been able to develop some iron-clad strategies to help anyone master this stage as well.

Your eSCORE is determined by analyzing the four stages of eSCAPE: self, catapult, authority, and people. Remember that you can find out what your eSCORE is by taking our free quiz at www.Lurn.com/quiz.

This quiz is made up of a series of very simple questions.

We ask you to tell us a bit about yourself and how you would react in certain situations. We need to get to know more about who you are, where you're coming from, and where you want to go.

At the end, you'll be given your eSCORE along with a full analysis of your rating in each of the four stages of S.C.A.P. The analysis not only reflects your overall probability of success in that moment, but it also dissects the exact ways you can increase your probability of achieving entrepreneurial success.

Our goal here is to get specific with you. It's nearly impossible to change yourself and grow if you have a *vague* idea of what you need. That's why we get precise and really hone in on specific areas with this quiz.

Drawing Conclusions From Your eSCORE

It's important to remember that this is just a standardized test. It's meant only to give you an idea of where you stand. It certainly is not meant to be the definitive answer to all of your questions.

I would never advise making a life decision purely off the number that a system, any system, gives to you.

Instead, read this book, do your best to understand all the core concepts and then weigh them with your eSCORE to build the full picture.

With that said, here's how I interpret the eSCORE:

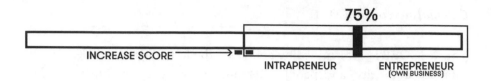

75%

INCREASE SCORE ➝

INTRAPRENEUR   ENTREPRENEUR
(OWN BUSINESS)

- Before you dive into starting your own business, try to make sure your eSCORE is at least above 75%.
- If your score is between 50% to 75%, you have two choices. Either a life as an *Intrapreneur* is going to be a great fit, or you can decide to study, train, and work on the weak links to improve your score.
- The further below 50% your eSCORE gets, the more you have to ask yourself whether becoming an Entrepreneur is right for you. Though the data will show that you have an uphill battle, it's still your choice.

You can think of your eSCORE as just one of many tools that you use to determine what the right career move is for you and your own unique situation.

Always remember that the decision you make is yours, nobody else's. There have been plenty of people throughout history who have been told they aren't good enough to do something, only to prove everyone wrong.

Now it's time to dive into each of the eSCAPE plan stages.

Let's start by taking a closer look at Stage 1—**Self**.

STAGE 1: SELF (S)

CHAPTER 8:
S—SELF

"Those who cannot change their minds cannot change anything."
– George Bernard Shaw

Remember that monumental failure I told you about in Chapter 1? The one where I went $1.7 million in debt and lost everything?

Well, this entire journey began when I was a college student. I went from having $100 in my pocket to building a business that was doing over $10 million a year, all within six years. I was on top of the world—or so I thought.

But here's the thing…

The more success I experienced, the less focused on **Self** I became and eventually, I paid a big price for it.

If you go back to when I first started my business, it was one of the most trying times of my life. In the first 18 months alone, I estimate that I failed over 50 times. However, I worked like crazy every single day until I finally had the breakthrough I needed. Honestly, now that I think about it, I was just using brute force and sheer willpower to make things happen.

Whatever it was, something had finally worked and I still remember the night I finally made my first $300. This was truly the moment that changed my life forever, I thought I would never look back from that.

From the first $300, I continued to repeat the same steps over and over, growing my first $300 night into generating over $10 million a year.

So, what did I do? I took the success I had and worked even harder to make my company bigger and better. This trained me to think that if I wanted to make more, I had to just work more. And for a while, my strategy worked like a charm.

However, unfortunately, bigger and better would eventually prove not to be the answer.

Beginning Of The End

Here's the thing about the initial success I had — *it wasn't really because of me*.

When I look back on that time, I can see that there were a number of environmental factors in play that I had given *myself* credit for. Granted, it definitely helped that I was a hard worker, but I can't ignore the fact that I was also operating in a market that was absolutely booming.

The reason this is important is because the minute the environment began to change, my business collapsed and everything came crashing down.

I realized later that I had really just built a house of cards. When it got too big, I wasn't prepared to handle it. So, it collapsed.

Why?

Because I failed at **Self**.

Self Is The Foundation Of Your Success

You can think of the four stages of S.C.A.P. as a pyramid, and Self is the base of that pyramid.

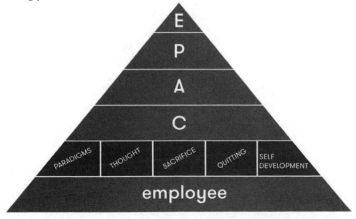

Self is at the base because it is the *foundation* of Entrepreneurial success. Nothing matters more than where your *mindset* is – it determines your decisions, actions, and ability to persevere.

Now that I look back, I can say with certainty that my mind was not in the right place. I had set up a false foundation of Self. Years later, when I had the chance to do a full analysis, I was able to lock down five particular elements of Self that make all the difference:

1. Paradigms
2. Power of Thought
3. Sacrifices
4. Quitting
5. Self-Development

With All Our Powers Combined

These five core elements are your armor against any of the challenges you may face as an Entrepreneur.

To better understand the inner workings of Self, let's start with the area in which I see many Entrepreneurs fail before they even begin. It's an area that has a lot to do with your past and other factors that you may not even know are in play.

It's called **paradigms.**

Let's dive in deeper.

CHAPTER 9:
PARADIGMS

"If you want small changes in your life, work on your attitude.
But if you want big and primary changes, work on your paradigm."
– Stephen Covey

I discovered the concept of paradigms when I was at my lowest point – $1.7 million in debt. I was beyond broke, my business was failing, my health was deteriorating, and even my relationships were falling apart.

I had literally hit my breaking point and I was only 27 years old!

So I had a choice on my hands. I could stand straight, face the music and fight, or I could cut the cord and run away. Fortunately, I chose to stand and fight.

The first step to fighting was to do a deep analysis to understand what exactly went wrong. Where did the tide turn? What was my role in this disaster? How could I make sure I didn't repeat the same mistakes? It was through this process that I came across a teaching from someone who went on to become one of my mentors - Bob Proctor. It felt like this one video from Bob literally reached out and smacked me across the face.

What I Learned From Bob Proctor

One of Bob's core teachings is a concept he calls "paradigms." The moment I saw him explain paradigms for me, it instantly made total sense.

For the first time, I could see a core foundational reason behind my failure.

So, what's a paradigm? Google it and the following definition comes up:

"A typical example or pattern of something; a model"

But, it goes way deeper than that. As Bob explains it, paradigms are a collection of habits that are embedded deep within the subconscious. These habits are created by coding and patterns that have been placed and reinforced inside of us for decades and decades.

All of our behavior, decisions, beliefs, loves, fears, and desires are controlled by this invisible force called your *paradigms.* So if you want to create success, you first need to dissect your past, understand your current paradigms, and if necessary, map a course to change your paradigms.

If your past paradigms are not in alignment with attracting success, you need to change them – there is no way around it. There's no skipping this step.

How Paradigms Develop

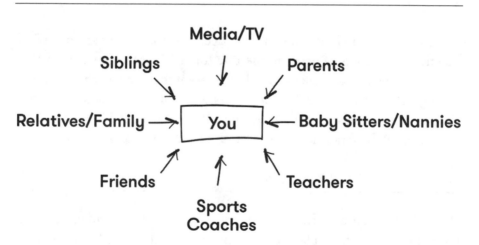

The patterns and models we use in our lives everyday were actually built *for us* when as we were growing up.

We had absolutely *no control* over the development of these paradigms. From the day we were born, everything we experienced in our childhood built our belief systems — whether these were joyful things or traumatic things or anything in between.

All of the memories from our childhood are constantly impacting the way we look at life and everything we do today.

And it's not just our childhood. It's also the people who have been around us our entire lives. These people unknowingly play a major role in the development of our behavior and belief patterns. This is the very reason why our parents' paradigms quickly become our paradigms. Our siblings' paradigms become our paradigms. Our teachers' paradigms become our paradigms.

Without even knowing it, we adopt the thinking systems of everyone around us and engrain them deep inside us. The question is, do we pick up the good patterns or the bad patterns?

Of course, we pick up a combination of both the good and bad patters. So, that leaves us with a suite of paradigms that need changing later in our lives, which leads to the main question…

How do we change our behavior and belief patterns after they've been buried so deep within our subconscious mind?

Turn To Physics: Newton's First Law

"An object at rest stays at rest, or an object in motion stays in motion at the same speed and in the same direction unless acted on by an unbalanced force."

Think of a paradigm as an object.

Now, imagine this object is moving in one direction, Newton's first law says that the object will continue to move in that direction indefinitely – the only way to stop the object or change it's direction would be by acting on it by an *unbalanced or opposing* force.

So, the only way to change what this object is doing is to act on it directly – you have to actively create the change.

Now, let's take the same thought process and apply it to the behaviors we repeat on a day to day basis. Apply it to our political beliefs. Apply it to our beliefs about dreams, money, relationships – you name it. The lesson here is that our current way of beliefs or our current cycles in life will continue to repeat over and over.

The only way to stop or change them would be to actively apply an opposing force, to actively work on them.

Change can only happen when you make a conscious effort to choose new beliefs that are aligned with the behaviors and habits you want to form. However, just choosing them is not enough. You must also take patient and daily action to reinforce these beliefs.

In other words, *you need to create a disturbance in the force…*

My Paradigm During the Greatest Fall of My LIFE

The six years of my Entrepreneurial journey after I made that first $300 was the equivalent of being attached to a rocket. I had little control. Mostly, I was just along for the ride. I was building and scaling my business with no formal training and truly had no idea what I was doing. At this point in my life, I had never even heard the word *paradigm*.

There was no way I could have self-reflected to see if there were any mind-traps in my journey. Instead, I just kept running forward, working through pure trial and error. I kept throwing things against the wall until something stuck, and then I held onto it for dear life.

Everything seemed to be going great on the surface, but that was actually the problem. I wasn't facing any challenges. My environment was completely static, so the same steps kept working, again and again.

However, things were about to change.

See, when your environment changes you really discover who you are. When everything around you changes, there's only one common element that can take control - you. So from then on out, as the market changed and the same steps were no longer working, it all came back to me.

Well, the *"me"* had a panic attack and started to melt.

Why?

This is when my paradigms, formed from the time I was a child, started rearing their ugly head.

Growing up, I had built deep feelings about *money*. Money was everything and seemed to be the solution to everything. People are fighting? Must be about money. Someone is upset or sad? Must be because of money. Major tension in the air? Must be the money. Someone is really happy? Yep. Money.

Listen, it's no one's fault. I grew up in a single-income middle class family in America. When I look back, I'm amazed how my father managed. We had a beautiful home, multiple cars, great food, and many other luxuries. But that's the thing, my father was wise with money. To be able to invest money in the areas that we needed it, my parents had to constantly say no to us when spending the money didn't make sense. And, of course my sister and I were demanding, so we heard the word "NO" a lot.

"No, we can't afford that. It costs too much."

"No, you don't need that."

These were all fair answers, but who knew that I was building a very interesting *relationship* with money because of it?

I remember making a commitment to myself when I was young that "When I grow up, I'm going to have so much money that I'll have no problems in my life. I'll be able to do whatever I want, buy whatever I want - period."

Although you may think this was a good commitment to make to myself, there are some serious flaws to that logic when you look deeper.

The paradigm that I had unknowingly built was that if there was ever a problem, I could throw money at it to make it go away. If there were good times, then spend that money and enjoy yourself. If there were bad times, throw money at them and make them go away.

I bet you're starting to see where I'm going with this and how these seemingly innocent beliefs nearly led me to the end of my life.

Dropping Revenue? Throw Some Money At It!

In early 2010, things started to take a horrific turn.

My revenue was plummeting. My expenses were out of control. We were bleeding money, and it was only getting worse and worse every month. I couldn't see any end in sight, but I had blind faith in myself. After all, everything I touched had turned to gold up until that point!

So in a place where most CEOs would start aggressively cutting costs and finding ways to optimize their revenue, here's what I did.

I threw money at it. Lots of it.

It's almost embarrassing to talk about it now, but I'm going to reveal it anyways.

- I hired more people.
- I expanded my offices.
- I spent more money on team culture activities.
- I decided to launch a new business model with no revenue proof.
- I started shutting down the lines that were generating revenue.
- I brought on expensive consultants to help me.

See what I mean? *I threw money at it.*

My decisions make no sense today, but they made perfect sense to me back then. Imagine, my money paradigms were so strong that I justified each of the above decisions and even convinced those around me to go along with me!

Everything had become about money.

Every project I did as I fell into debt about the money. Every problem I had - borrow and invest more money. Every decision I had to make - give someone else money and have them make it.

My relationship with money had become the greatest poison in my life.

I Had To Change My Paradigms

Obviously, I had to change these paradigms to recover. I had to completely *rewrite* them. I turned back to reading, meditating, and reflecting on who I was and who I wanted to become.

It took me weeks to fully realize just how much my paradigms had impacted my entire life. However, I didn't have more weeks to change them.

So, I had to do something drastic. I decided to turn to good ole physics. Newton's first law spoke of applying an opposing force, so that's just what I did. I realized that too many of the decisions I had made were *money-*related, so I took some drastic steps to counter.

1. I shut down many lines of products that I didn't believe in even though they made good money.
2. I went from a team of near 100 people down to a team of 6.
3. I eliminated expenses - even ones that I swore I couldn't run my company without.

After that, I made a declaration to myself:

> *"I will only sell products that I truly believe in. I will absolutely NOT do any project just for the money, and I won't hire anyone just to solve a problem."*

The first few months were very, very painful.

However, I stuck to it. I meditated on the new paradigms that I wanted to create every single night:

87

1. *Money is irrelevant*—The key is to love what you're doing and feel a true passion.
2. *It's all about strategy, planning, and having contingency plans*—Make wise decisions, not gutsy ones.
3. *Serve those in need* —It's NOT about the money; it's about the people.

I found that these were the exact messages I needed to hear over and over again. Honestly, it didn't take nearly as long as I had suspected for my paradigms to shift to my new ways of thinking.

I then started a new line of products that I absolutely loved and I knew from which my students could get results.

Here's what happened:

- In 16 months, I had paid back $1.7 million in debt.
- My first passion project went on to generate over $3 million in its first year.
- My health recovered.
- I was back in business and climbing to the top.
- I found fulfillment and happiness.

My growth hasn't stopped since then.

I'm constantly re-emphasizing my adjusted paradigm, and it has served me tremendously well. I've kept a strong relationship with money that never has me relying on it.

My focus remains on my actions and how they impact others. It's incredible what a little adjustment can do in an Entrepreneur's life.

Question Time

Now it's your turn, and it's important to be honest with yourself. Ask yourself the following questions:

- What are your paradigms in life?
- What do you believe about yourself?
- What do you believe about success?
- What do you believe about being an Entrepreneur?
- What do you believe you are worthy of having?
- What do you believe you are capable of?

These paradigms play a HUGE role behind the scenes of your life, but you're the director. You can take control of the paradigms and change them for the better, if you analyze them carefully.

When you answer these questions, you have to be completely honest with yourself. This is the ONLY way you will be able to see them for what they are so that you can change them.

Now, let me ask you a blunt question. Do you BELIEVE you have what it takes to succeed? Or has your past taught you otherwise?

This is perhaps the most important question you can ask yourself. If you don't actually believe you can succeed deep down, not a single other thing in this book can help you.

You have to start there.

To explain more, let's move on to talking about the power of thought.

CHAPTER 10:
THE POWER OF THOUGHT
AND SELF-TALK

"Nothing can stop the man with the right mental attitude from achieving his goal; nothing on earth can help the man with the wrong mental attitude."
– Thomas Jefferson

"What if this launch fails? What if I fail *again*? What if I keep losing money?"

These were the thoughts going through my head in 2011, back when I was barreling down the road to failure. These thoughts plagued me every waking moment of my life.

I was surrounded by this self-talk of *what if I fail?*

Guess what happened? I ended up failing.

Ironically, all of my worst fears came true. Coincidence? I highly doubt it.

Fast forward for a moment to much happier times in 2017. This was a year of major growth and success for my business and personal life - arguably the best year of my life. If you took a quick snapshot of my mind at any given time in 2017, here were my inner thoughts and self-talk:

"What's my next move as we continue to grow? Where do I invest next to grow faster? How do I handle all this growth? What's the next dream I want to attack?"

See the difference?

That day in 2013 when I sat in my closed office, late at night, trying to figure out what went wrong, I had one major realization. I realized that night that I had gone from being an ambitious and positive person to a bitter and negative person. Once I realized and accepted that, I committed myself to experiencing a complete shift in my thinking. I needed to get back to my roots.

With nothing more than a strong declaration and a little focus, my thoughts became far more positive, hopeful, and eager. Again, it's not coincidence that I started making better decisions, executing faster, and had a clearer mind.

So what's the science behind it? How did my change in thought become a change in action?

Explaining Thought With Science

There are many terms in the personal development world to explain the concept behind thoughts and self-talk. You've probably heard them before: law of attraction, manifestation, etc. Well, for a minute, let's explore the actual scientific explanation.

We have a part of our brain called the reticular activating system (RAS). It sounds fancy, but it's nothing more than a group of nerves located at the base of the brain stem—a very important group of nerves. The role of the RAS is to make sure our brain doesn't get short circuited from all the data that goes into it every second of the day.

Essentially, the RAS acts as a filter. Whenever something comes into the brain through one or more of our senses, the RAS determines if this is a piece of information that is important enough to bring to our attention. If it's not, we take no notice of it.

For example, if you're in a crowded room and people are talking all around you, the RAS will filter out all the *noise*. Everything is loud and the brain registers none of it. BUT if someone happens to say your name from across the room, suddenly the RAS recognizes the importance of that word and immediately lets it through. Before you know it, in a loud room where you couldn't hear a thing, you're now jolting back and forth looking for the person who said your name.

Here's another great example.

Let's say you go car shopping. You walk into a dealership and there she is, a beautiful car right in front of you. You immediately react and your mind is thinking, "Wow! I love this car! I've never seen it before." You love it so much that you take the car for a test drive and spend an hour asking questions as you flip through the brochure.

You tell the salesperson that you'll think on it and be back later. You leave the dealership. You don't even realize it, but your entire RAS has been reshaped in that last hour.

As soon as you pull out of the car lot, you look in your rear-view mirror and, "*WOAH! There's the same car behind me!*" As you keep driving and turn into your neighborhood, there it is again. It's parked in your neighbor's driveway.

You can't help but think, "*Wow. This car has gotten so popular all of a sudden!*" However, the truth is that the car was always there. The car isn't what's new. You noticing it is what's new. Before you went to the dealership, it was just random noise for your RAS, so it got filtered out. However, the car suddenly has your attention and the RAS is letting it through.

Your awareness and focus on a subject is actually creating your experience in reality.

Now, hold that thought...

The RAS And Success

The RAS is crucial to reaching success in life. They key is to tune your RAS into the things you want to accomplish - through focus, attention, and prioritization.

You see, the one person you talk to the most every day is yourself. That little voice is constantly chattering away. Whether you like it or not, it has your focus, attention, and prioritization. This is precisely why aligning the voice with what you want to achieve is absolutely imperative.

Just do a quick test on yourself right now. Measure your inner voice. Would you say that it's a positive influence in your life or a negative one? I can tell you right now that odds are it's not a very positive voice.

It's just human nature. We're trained to be skeptical, suspicious, and generally negative. But for a minute, imagine that you keep your inner voice positive, uplifting, and hopeful throughout the day.

How would that directly impact your day?

The science is simple; changing your inner dialogue will instantly train your RAS to tune you into decisions and action that are in alignment with your goals. Your RAS can actually become your most powerful ally.

So, how do you train your thoughts and self-talk? What if I said that you don't actually have to do anything? That it's easier to change your inner dialogue by not doing anything *directly*?

The simple truth is that trying to use the conscious to change the subconscious is largely a waste of time, so I actually prefer a much sneakier approach.

The Power Of Pictures & Words

December 22, 2017 - I walked into a local church group and the entire living room was full of magazines, colors, pens, scissors, and poster boards. *"What in the world is going on here?"* As I walked in, everyone was incredibly energized and buzzing about how they were going to be working on their 2018 *dream boards* that night.

Honestly, I could have leapt six feet in the air with joy. Dream boards! Who told them about my secret weapon to making my biggest goals come true?

Dream boards are visual representations of your goals and priorities. You can include pictures, words, colors, anything that inspires you and puts you in the mindset you're trying to achieve.

My process for creating a dream board was simple.

I found a quiet corner of the house and made a list of all my goals. Nothing was off the table. If my heart desired it, it was on the list.

I covered the following categories:

- Spiritual
- Health
- Relationships
- Wealth
- Philanthropy
- Materialistic

By the time I was done with the exercise, I had 16 goals written down. Yes, 16. And not a cell in my body had any doubt. I knew that if I kept my focus on them, each and every one was achievable.

Now, here's the blunt truth. What I had on my dream board for 2018 was more ambitious than most people would have on their dream boards for their *entire life*. This was another moment of pride for me - I knew that I had truly grown in my ability to dream big and focus big.

Here are some examples of what made it to my dream board:

- Raise $1 million in donations *(notice how it is a specific number)*.
- Speak in front of 5,000+ people.
- Open the first Lurn Center.
- Lose 30 pounds.
- Earn $500,000 through day trading.
- Invest 15 minutes a day into praying.

That was just a small sample of the goals on my 2018 dream board. So, what happened?

As soon as January 1 hit, I made sure my dream board was my top focus. Here are a few things I did to give my dream board more exposure in my daily life.

1. I got multiple copies of the poster board printed to use in both my home and office.
2. I changed the background on my phone and computer to an image of my dream board.
3. I spent at least one minute a day looking at it.
4. I kept the written list folded in my wallet.
5. I shared my board with my wife and instantly built accountability.

I couldn't believe it.

Just 3 months later, five of the 16 dreams had already come true. In just 3 months, I had finished nearly 33% of the goals on my dream board, and it felt as if it was almost effortless.

Opportunities had miraculously come about. A dream I had for over 13 years came true in a matter of weeks, and it wasn't some stroke of luck or crazy voodoo. I could clearly see what had led to my success. I was making better decisions. My focus was laser tight, and I was constantly thinking about my dreams. My attitude was upbeat, hopeful, and excited.

I couldn't believe the impact just one poster board and small piece of paper in my wallet had on my life.

So, here's why this works so well.

As you surround yourself with your dream board and dream list, you're "*tricked*" into seeing it many times throughout the day. You can't help but bring your focus to it repeatedly. So instead of getting lost in some of those negative thoughts that you might have throughout the day, you steal a glance at your dream board to bring your thoughts back to the positivity that you want to bring into your life.

You're also constantly communicating with your RAS and letting it know that these are the things that are the most important to you. Again, recode your RAS and it'll automatically start helping you make better decisions.

There you have it.

The best and most effortless way to recode your inner thoughts and inner talk, one picture at a time.

Question Time

And now it's time to ask yourself a few questions:

- *What are some of your limiting beliefs?* Really think about what your beliefs are and why you have them.
- *Do you say one thing and your mind immediately says the opposite?* For example, if you say, "I'm going to lose 20 pounds," pay attention to the voice in your head right after you say it. Is it saying, "Heck yeah. Let's do this!" Or is it saying, "Whatever."
- *Do you believe good things or bad things are happening to you?* Take a current snapshot of your life. Do you think you are a fortunate person who should be grateful, or do you think everyone else has it better than you?

With that said, I have a very revealing exercise for you. This is a simple test, but you have to be COMPLETELY honest with yourself for it to work.

I want you to track your thoughts for just a day.

- Grab a piece of paper and draw a line down the middle.
- On the left side, write, "Negative."
- On the right side, write, "Positive."
- Now, track yourself as best as you can throughout the day.
- Every time you have a positive thought, one where you feel good or feel a buzz, put a mark in the positive column.
- Every time you have a negative thought that results in fear, frustration, or anger, put a mark in the negative column.

At the end of the day, count the total number of marks, both negative and positive.

There you have it. Which category won?

Just divide the total positive marks with the total number of marks all together and you'll have a percentage. You'll know, mathematically, just how positive a person you are.

I cannot stress enough how important this exercise is.

Moving on, you'll see why it's so imperative for you to keep your focus squarely on your goals. The next step to becoming an Entrepreneur is not easy, but it can quickly become less painful if you have constant reminders of your focus.

Let's talk about *making sacrifices.*

CHAPTER 11:
SACRIFICES

"Great achievement is usually born of great sacrifice,
and is never the result of selfishness."
– Napoleon Hill

House parties, football games, lazy days on campus.

If you're like most people, that's how you imagine the American college experience, and you really wouldn't be far from the truth. In fact, maybe you even lived this college life yourself.

However, my college years were far from parties and football games.

While I was certainly tempted to indulge in all of the enjoyable and fun parts of college, I just couldn't bring myself to do it.

Why?

My desire to become successful was so strong at that time that I couldn't physically force myself to focus on anything other than building my business.

To give you an idea of what I mean, this is what my typical day looked like in college:

- I would wake up at 7:00 or 7:30 a.m., just in time to make it to class at 8:00 or 8:30 a.m.
- During many of my classes, I would rarely take notes or pay attention. Instead, I was on my laptop working on things related to my online business. I was on forums, checking my email, reading, catching up on what was happening, and making sure that I didn't miss a single opportunity.
- At lunch, I would purposely avoid anyone I knew so I could do classwork while I was eating. That way, I had no distractions while I worked on major assignments or crammed for a test.

- When classes were done at around 2:00 or 3:00 p.m., I would head back to my dorm and do classwork for approximately two hours.
- Since I was a financial planner during my college days, I would head out around 4:00 p.m., drive for 45 minutes to the company office and meet with clients. The meetings were always in the evenings.
- The client meetings would finish around 7:00 or 8:00 p.m. I would then drive back to my apartment and give myself about 45 minutes to eat and unwind in front of the TV or hang out with my roommates.
- From around 10:00 p.m. to about 2:00 a.m., I would work on my online business. Then I would get up the next day and start the cycle all over again.

Why am I telling you this? Because you need to see what it means to sacrifice short-term gratification for long-term success.

In college, I sacrificed almost all of the fun things that everyone else was doing because I was so focused on building something that would set me up for life. In those days, I only let myself catch up on sleep ONE day of the week: Sunday.

My weekends were more of the same.

I refused to waste time going to bars and lounges. You'd never see me at a basketball or football game. I didn't join social clubs.

My dreams were *everything* to me, so I invested every waking minute that I had into working toward them.

So, did it pay off?

I'll leave that for you to decide.

Understanding Sacrifice

The word "sacrifice" has a very bad reputation. This is due in part to the definition you get when you look up *sacrifice* in the dictionary:

"...an act of slaughtering an animal or person or surrendering a possession as an offering to God or to a divine or supernatural figure."

Slaughtering? Death? Oh my...

No wonder the thought of sacrifice leads to such horrible reactions. Well, I see it in a completely different light. For me, sacrifice is an opportunity. I look at sacrifice as a positive *choice* I get to make to prioritize my dreams.

Sacrifice is actually a very simple concept.

We have 24 hours in a day. That's it. There's nothing you can do to get any more time, period. So we start there. Now we have to work backwards and figure out how to *use* this time.

Doctors say we should sleep eight hours a day. So, there goes eight. That leaves us with 16 hours in a day. If you think about it, that's a lot of time.

I want you to think for a moment about how you use those 16 hours. Do you *invest* this time into your future and your dreams or do you *spend* this time and trade it in for immediate enjoyment.

In college, I definitely missed out on a lot.

There were many days when I felt alone or sad because I knew that all my friends were out having a blast. And me? I was locked in my dorm banging away at my keyboard.

But look at me today.

Because I always felt that I was in control, I now get to live the life of my dreams.

We Are All Capable of Sacrifice

Sacrifice is simple.

It's just about making choices.

Just like you choose to drink hot or cold water or you choose to wear jeans or sweatpants, you choose whether or not you're going to make sacrifices in your life to get what you want.

Remember, sacrificing isn't about being unreasonable or forcing yourself to endure pain in order to reach success. It's just about how you choose to use your limited time on this planet.

And every single second counts.

I say that because your choices directly shape what the future holds for you.

Are you willing to give up your TV time? Are you willing to give up your happy hours at the local bar? Are you willing to give up eating out to save money for your business? Are you willing to buy an older car so that you can spend more money on educating, building, and investing in yourself?

See that? It's just about choices.

The number one question I get asked all the time is, "Anik, what's the formula for success?"

My answer to those people is actually pretty simple. It's just math. You have a limited number of hours and seconds in this world, so how are you using them? The activities that you choose to invest the most time in determine what you'll get.

So, the formula?

Invest as much of your free time as you can into fighting for your dreams. Whether you're investing that time into reading, studying, taking courses, finding mentorship or actually executing a plan, it's bringing you that much closer to your dreams.

That's what I mean by sacrifice.

Doesn't sound so bad, right?

Map out your day. What does it look like between the hours of 5:00 p.m. and 12:00 a.m.? These are typically "non-work hours." What are you choosing to spend your time doing?

Are you watching TV or surfing Facebook? Or are you doing something to move toward your dreams?

Next question.

What is one thing that you currently sacrifice in your life to invest into your dreams? I want you to make a list of these sacrifices. Get them all out on paper and be HONEST.

If you can't think of much, no problem. Don't feel bad. The point of this exercise is to recognize areas in which you can make improvements.

I really want you to think about your answers to these questions. If you're spending your time watching TV or on Facebook and can't list any sacrifices, then this might be a good place to start increasing your eSCORE.

After all, you have to get started somewhere.

CHAPTER 12:
QUITTING

"I'm convinced that about half of what separates the successful entrepreneurs from the non-successful ones is pure perseverance."
– Steve Jobs

"Anik, there's only one way. Declare bankruptcy and we can buy time to fix this."

These were the words of my lawyer when my business was failing and I was $1.7 million in debt.

As I walked out of his office, I was absolutely torn inside. I knew my lawyer was coming from a good place. He really wanted to help me, but I couldn't shake the thought, "Am I going to go through the rest of my life knowing I quit? Or am I going to dive in even harder and have faith in my ability to recover from this?"

Did I really want to be the type of person who throws in the towel? Did I want to go back on my word to all those who I owed money? Did I really want to give up and quit after going through so much?

It's not like this was the first time I had failed. I had fallen down many times in my life before and had gotten up and prevailed every single time.

I knew I had a choice in front of me—be the person who quits or the person who has enough faith to push on even harder. I just didn't know which I was going to choose.

As I stepped off the elevator that day, heading out of my lawyer's office, a memory replayed itself in my mind. It had easily been a decade since I had last thought about it...

I remembered the red door — a moment when I was a child that truly defined the rest of my life.

When I was younger, our school would host a giftwrapping fundraiser every year. The school would give all of the students catalogues of wrapping paper, and we would go out and try to sell to friends, family, and neighbors. The funds we raised would go to a charitable cause and the students would win amazing prizes for helping.

For some reason, even though I was a shy kid, I always did very well this time of year. Over the course of a few years, I had built up some pretty loyal customers in my neighborhood. So I decided that my fifth grade year was going to be the year that I finished number one in the contest and won the top prize.

I had an entire plan of action.

I had done the math as to how I would become number one. As long as my usual customers bought from me, I had a great chance at being the top salesman. In my mind, all I needed to do was *show up*.

Unfortunately, my plans started shattering the moment I knocked on my first door.

Within the first hour, I had been up one entire street in my neighborhood and not one of my past customers had bought from me. They all courteously declined. It made no sense! Not even one person wanted to help out a little fifth grader? What was going on?

I had knocked on at least eight or nine doors and had long and pleasant conversations, but every single person said no.

I remember standing there after the last rejection, completely deflated. My plan was shot, and there was literally no chance of me winning the top prize.

If I wasn't going to win, what was the point of continuing?

I was just about to turn around and retreat back to my house with my head hung low in self-pity when, suddenly, something bright in the distance caught my attention...

I saw the house with the red door.

They were the new neighbors. They'd just moved in, and the entire neighborhood was talking about how they had painted their front door and shutters this hideous bright red. I stood there looking at the house with the red door and figured, *"Why not go over and try? I'm here anyway. Maybe I can meet the new neighbors. Plus it's embarrassing that I have zero sales, so let's see if I can get at least something."*

I knocked on the red door and a very nice lady with a huge smile opened the door. I can still remember her kind face and sweet voice. I said, "Hi, I'm from the local elementary school and I'm selling gift wrapping paper. I was wondering if you would like to buy some?"

I couldn't believe what happened next.

As it turned out, this lady volunteered at the local church and had recently been tasked with buying all the wrapping paper the church needed for that Christmas season. Even though the wrapping paper I was selling was more expensive than what was available at the local market, she bought *25 rolls* on the spot!

During the walk back from her house to mine I remember thinking, *"Now what if I had quit? I stood right here thinking of turning back. But just because I knocked on one more door, look what happened!*

So, the lesson to learn?

Every house that said no before the red door got me closer to a yes. Every time someone said no, the probability the next person said yes went up.

I never forgot that lesson and, as it turns out, many before me have learned the same lesson too.

It's Simple Statistics

You see, all of this comes down to statistics.

In all honesty, I'm always shocked by how we don't innately understand this concept. Assume you're about to try something where the odds are against you. I mean the odds of you succeeding are very small.

When are your odds of success better? If you give it everything you've got and TRY, or if you get discouraged and never try to begin with?

Think about it.

Even if you only have a 1% chance of success, showing up and trying means you have that 1% chance of success. It might not be much, but it's something. Quitting, or never even trying at all, *guarantees* you a 0% chance of success.

Thus, the odds are in your favor when you at least show up.

Think about flipping a coin.

Let's assume that you flip a coin multiple times. Somehow, every flip is landing on tails. Flip after flip, you keep seeing tails. Well, statistically, your odds are changing with every flip. The chances of you finally getting heads are going up more and more aggressively with every flip.

Just think of that in the context of sales. If you keep trying and learning, you're statistically getting closer to a yes every time you hear a no. It's just math.

Did you know Thomas Edison made *1,000 failed attempts* when he was creating the lightbulb? What would our world be like if he had quit?

J.K. Rowling was rejected by 12 different publishers before she found one who would publish the first *Harry Potter* book. Where would children's literature be if she had quit?

Sylvester Stallone's script for *Rocky* was rejected more than 1,000 times. When he was finally made an offer, it was only on the condition that he wouldn't star in the movie. He refused. He took a mere $35,000 in pay, plus a percentage of the profits, just to star in his own movie. That first movie went on to make $200 million at the box office.

Can you imagine a world without Rocky?

There are dozens of these stories out there. Why? Because it's the truth. The only way to fail is to stop trying. Quitting is failure. Everything before you quit is just a part of your journey.

This actually means that failure is a choice.

You choose to fail when you quit.

Question Time

Now it's time for you to do some soul searching. Here are some questions to help you along the way.

Think back to the last time you QUIT something — a diet, a business, a New Year's resolution—anything. Ask yourself:

- What could you have done differently?
- Exactly WHY did you quit? Did you lose motivation? Was it too hard? Did you fail and then just fizzle out? Were you too afraid? Was it because of the people around you?
- What if, instead of throwing in the towel, you had what I call a *"whiteboard moment?"* What if you had asked yourself, "Why am I failing so much? What can I learn from this failure, and what can I do differently?"

It's so important to know WHY you quit!

You really need to take the time to dive into this because this is where you will learn quite a bit about yourself and where you need to improve. This is where your opportunity for self-development will come through.

And self-development is what we are going to talk about next because it's critical to success in ANY area of life.

CHAPTER 13:
SELF-DEVELOPMENT -
THE SECRET OF BILLIONAIRES

"Formal Education will make you a living;
self-education will make you a fortune."
– Jim Rohn

When I was in high school, I constantly observed everything around me.

I took it all in.

My cousin was becoming a doctor, and my family has a lot of respect for people who become doctors. They make lots of money, drive nice cars, have big houses, and get a lot of praise.

Many parts of me connected success with becoming a doctor and so I was pretty certain that becoming a doctor was my future.

However, at the same time, I couldn't shake this weird feeling that there was a different path for me. I kept feeling like I wanted to do my own thing. Something that maybe my family wouldn't understand. This concept of total freedom became ingrained in my mind very early on, and I have no idea why.

The feeling became so strong that I actually skipped class one day, got in my car and drove to the local bookstore. I was on a mission to find a book that could help explain this inner conundrum.

Was I to become a doctor or was there another way? I was browsing the book shelves when one particular book caught my eye.

That was the day I found the book that changed my life.

I don't know what made me grab that book.

I guess the title was catchy.

Whatever it was, I pulled *Rich Dad, Poor Dad* off the shelf and started reading it right there in the store. I realized pretty quickly that there was something to this book. I connected with it instantly.

I didn't have much money back then, but I had just enough saved up to buy the book, so I did. I took it home and read it all the way through in just two days.

That was officially the first book I ever read from cover to cover.

When I was finished, I remember putting the book down and saying, *"Man, this is what I've been saying. This what I've been thinking. This is what I've been feeling."*

It changed my life.

No, I didn't run out and become an Entrepreneur right away. I just had the confirmation of a feeling. Unfortunately, it wasn't nearly enough to change my career or path at that time. I still went on to study pre-med in college and started my journey to become a doctor.

It didn't take long in college for me to realize that I was on the wrong path. In fact, I was miserable. Something had to change.

It was then that I dug through boxes to find the book again. I sat down one Saturday night and plowed through the book again and even ran to the bookstore around midnight to grab another book from the same author called *Cashflow Quadrant*.

That ended up being the book that did it for me.

Finally, I had a complete answer.

The fact that I now had an answer was the good news. However, the bad news right behind it was this "answer" had just dropped a one-ton bomb right in the middle of my life. I'm very grateful for this book as it started a chain reaction in my life that allowed to be where I am today.

So, the moral of the story? I can confidently say that all my success began the day I I chose to read a BOOK.

The Most Successful People Read—A LOT

Today, when I look around my kitchen, my bedroom or my office, I see books everywhere. In fact, the one thing my wife yells at me the most about is when she constantly trips over my collection of what she calls "millionaire books."

I'm an avid reader and I devour books, sometimes on a daily basis.

I get excited just thinking about the infinite amount of knowledge that sits within steps of where I am. There's spiritual knowledge, relationship knowledge, health knowledge, business knowledge, technical knowledge - there's literally an answer to almost any question you might have.

I've also seen a direct correlation between my pace of reading and the acceleration of my success both in business and in several other areas of my life. The more I see it, the more excited I am to read every day.

I'm not the only one who has noticed this correlation between reading and wealth.

Steve Siebold, a broke college student, was plagued with a question for years. "*How does someone become rich?*" So, he decided to find the answer. He set out on a mission to interview as many successful people as he could find.

To date, he's interviewed over 1,200 of the wealthiest people in the world.

And guess what he found?

He discovered a common trait that almost every person he interviewed shared - they ALL read books, lots of books.

- Mark Cuban—Reads more than three hours per day.
- Bill Gates—Reads about one book per week.
- Warren Buffet—Devotes five to six hours of his work day to reading.
- Oprah Winfrey—Loves reading so much she chooses one book she has read each month for her Book Club members to read.
- Elon Musk—Credits learning how to build rockets to reading books.
- Tony Robbins—Spends at least 30 minutes a day reading.

Does reading really make that much of a difference?

Tom Corley spent five years studying the habits and attitudes of rich and poor people and here's what he found:

- 88% of wealthy people read at least 30 minutes a day, but only 2% of poor people read at least 30 minutes a day.
- 86% of wealthy people love to read and only 26% of poor people love to read.
- 85% of wealthy people read two or more educational books per month, compared to only 15% of poor people.
- 63% of wealthy people listen to audiobooks while commuting, compared to only 5% of poor people.

The data is irrefutable.

The best thing you can do for your journey to wealth is to start reading as much as possible.

Yet I Had STOPPED Reading

One of the biggest things I noticed about myself when I was dissecting what happened when I fell $1.7 million in debt was how my reading habits had changed.

I had stopped reading.

I had stopped taking courses. I had stopped learning. I was too busy living the high life to devote any time to self-education.

In my mind, I guess I thought I was already there. When I dissected my business to see why I had failed, I realized I couldn't remember the last book I had read. During the six years I was building my business, I read anything and everything given to me - even on top of a full reading load from college.

I had no room or time for excuses. Yet when my life was falling apart I couldn't think of a single book I had read in at least two years!

That was when I realized that the day you stop learning is the day you start dying.

The night I realized this, I remember rushing home and running straight to our bookshelf. It didn't matter what book I chose, I just needed to spend hours that night reading. I had to get back to my habit.

Since that night, I never stopped reading and my life "miraculously" turned around.

Still Reading Today

Yes, I still read today—probably more than ever.

I try to read at least one book per week.

Even if I don't make that goal, I almost always read at least 35 books a year. When I can't actually read a book, I listen to them on Audible. Time is not an issue. I listen to books when I'm in the shower, when I'm driving, when I'm flying and even during commercials on TV. Any free time I find, I try to invest it into reading or listening.

In fact, I don't just focus on books. I'm veracious about taking online courses on topics that interest me, going to seminars, paying for coaches and even getting private mentoring.

In 2017, I estimated how much I had invested in self-education. It came out to nearly $250,000 between books, courses, coaches, and consultants. That may sound like a lot of money, but you can't even begin to imagine how much I made from that investment.

The impact is just incredible.

My Reading Formula

I think all books are exciting and wonderful. The bookstore is FULL of knowledge on so many subjects.

But the books I like to read can be broken down into four categories:

1. Spiritual
2. Health
3. Wealth
4. Relationships

Every few months, I change my season of learning. I pick something I really want to focus on at that particular time, and then I rotate between the categories every few months.

The year I got married, 2014, I immediately dove in and chose the *relationship* category as my focus for a few months. I read everything I could about relationships, marriage, and communication. Let me tell you something, it made a world of a difference.

After that, I switched over to the *wealth* category because I wanted to see faster growth in my business. I started taking courses on topics I needed to master. It's no coincidence that the second half of 2014 saw some of the fastest growth I had ever experienced as an Entrepreneur.

Fast forward to today.

My focus is currently on the *health* category. In all my years of aggressively focusing on my business, I realized that I've let my health slide, so I decided to make a change.

In just two months of focusing on health, I'm down 15 pounds and feeling five times better. Again, this isn't coincidence or luck. This is all happening by design.

When you read and self-educate, you can make an *immediate* impact on your life.

The secret of the truly wealthy and successful people in this world is the simplest of them all—pick up a book and spend a lot of time reading!

Question Time

I only have one question for you in this chapter, and I want you to think about it carefully.

How much time each day do you invest in improving yourself?

I don't care if you're taking a course, watching videos, reading a book, or working with a coach. How much time do you invest, every single day, in improving yourself?

I honestly believe that there's no chance of you succeeding as an Entrepreneur if reading and self-educating aren't habits in your life.

So, grab a book and start reading!

Once you've begun to change your mindset about self-education, you'll be ready to start moving forward as an Entrepreneur. That will lead you to the next stage of your Entrepreneurial development.

I call this stage *Catapult.*

STAGE 2: CATAPULT (C)

CHAPTER 14:
C – CATAPULT

"Momentum begets momentum, and the best way to start is to start."
– Gil Penchina

I very clearly remember the first business I started.

It was 1998 and home computers were still a relatively new thing. The idea of having someone come to your home and fix your computer wasn't really available in our area. You had to unplug your computer, drag it to your car and find a shop. Even then, it was always in some shady corner of a strip mall.

It was fertile ground for a young Entrepreneur, and I ALMOST seized the opportunity.

While eating lunch one day in high school, I was eavesdropping on a conversation between two teachers, as young students often do.

Their conversation was fascinating.

They both seemed to be at their wit's end with their home computers and they spent their entire lunch talking about how many problems they had with them. However, it wasn't until the very end that they said something that stopped me dead in my tracks.

"Wouldn't it be great if we could pay someone to come over, fix our computer for good and just be done with it? I'd be willing to pay good money for that."

The other teacher emphatically agreed and, from there, the rest of my day was shot. I spent the next few classes scribbling calculations in my notebook and planning my attack.

A home computer repair service was a BRILLIANT idea at that time.

As I scribbled my notes throughout the day, I also realized that I had the perfect asset for the project. I didn't know a thing about computers back then, but it didn't matter because I happened to have a great friend who was a computer genius!

I chased him down at the end of school before he could board his bus and immediately went to work on him. I used my slickest sales techniques and he agreed to partner with me within a few minutes. Just like that, I had my first business partner.

Now, with as much planning as I did, there were a few core things I forgot. For one, my friend was a freshman in high school. He was about 14 years old and couldn't drive. I was only 15 at the time, so I couldn't drive him either.

So our first problem was transportation, but we had an even bigger problem. As minors, I didn't even know if it was legal for us to start a business.

That sure as heck wasn't going to hold me back!

I had absolutely no idea what I was doing. The only strategy I had was some chicken scratch in the back of my math notebook, and I couldn't even read most of it by the next day. No matter what plans I thought I had created, here's what I really had to start with:

- No experience.
- No idea how to work with computers.
- No clients.
- No knowledge of how to get clients.
- No way to actually drive to the homes of these clients.
- No idea what and how to charge.
- No clue if minors being in business was even legal.

Look at all of those no's.

Even ONE of these facts would be enough to stop many people from pursuing their dreams. However, it didn't even register for me. As a matter of fact, I purposely didn't ask my parents because I knew they'd just say, *"You're too young. Focus on school."*

So, I had this brilliant business idea and a great business partner. It was time to conquer the next biggest challenge —*how to get customers.*

"How Much Is An Ad In Your Newspaper?"

"Need customers? Place an ad somewhere. Where? The newspaper! Absolutely genius!"

That evening, I called *The Gazette*, our local city newspaper. I spoke to the saleslady there and took notes on how to place an ad in their newspaper. I had no money or plan for placing the ad, but I wanted to do my background research.

However, the only way the lady could price the ad for me was to actually write it, put it into the system and see. So I did what any great Entrepreneur does. I wrote the ad on the spot, using my friend's real name and number, so that she could give me a price.

I still remember what she quoted me. It was $180. Back in 1998, for a broke high school kid with no job, this was like asking for a million dollars.

I told her I would call back, hung up and added another challenge to the list. I knew that the ad was worth it because having just one customer would cover the cost of the ad. So, now my mission had become to find $180. Again, I had no idea how I would do it, but I knew I would figure it out.

As it turned out, the lady forgot to delete the ad from the system.

A week later, I came home from school still trying to figure out how to hustle $180 from somewhere when my "business partner" called me in pure panic. "What did you do?! Our phone won't stop ringing and strange people keep asking if we can fix their computers! Dude, my mom is livid. She's really angry. What did you do?"

The entire time he was talking, all I could think was, *"Wow, it worked! We're going to be rich!"*

I talked him off the ledge and helped him understand that it was a happy accident and that we were now officially in business. I had just unlocked a system that could get us as many customers as we could ever want. This was good news! I said, "Call them all back right away, book them and I'll find a way to get you to their house."

Well, that first venture was very short-lived. I wasn't done with my sentence before his mom picked up the other line and absolutely declined. There was no way her son was going to do any of this. No business. No customers. No going to people's houses. Absolutely not.

"We had a good run," I thought. Time to close our doors. Hey, at least I learned a bit about how newspaper ads run. At least I took action. I didn't know what I was doing, but I turned it into multiple prospective customers!

I thought I got away with the free ad. That is, until a bill came in the mail the following week. My dad threw the bill on the table and just said, "Now what did you do?"

Luckily, the ad truly did end up being free. My dad actually laughed about the whole thing. He called the newspaper, explained how they had just sold a service to a minor and the bill disappeared instantly.

Although it died before it even got started, that business *could* have taken off. Maybe I could have even sold it for millions! The point is, I took action. I built momentum.

I didn't have a clue what I was doing, but I was able to turn an idea into so many prospects that the phone wouldn't stop ringing. I learned a very valuable lesson from that business.

Who cares if you don't know what to do? The key is to DO.

You can figure out the details as you go.

I realized early on in my life that one of my greatest gifts was that I didn't look for perfection. I didn't care for plans. I get excited, think of ideas, and run after them at 100 mph.

I pivot as I run. I make changes as I learn.

Many times, I fail and fall. That never stops me.

Even today, the word *perfection* has no place in my life. Most people waste their entire lives waiting for the *perfect plan*. An Entrepreneur just wants to start running and creating momentum. They want to remain nimble and adapt as they go.

The bottom line is that they want to *go*. No waiting around. No learning. No excuses.

Just start and create momentum.

The Real Issue Is Fear

Let's talk about perfection a bit more.

Is the idea of perfection what's really stopping people from taking action toward their dreams? Deep down, do we really care about having the perfect plan? My bet is on...NO.

Actually, most of us couldn't care less about the plan. We barely plan anything else in our lives, so why would we be so attached to a plan now?

Well, it's simple.

We're attracted to the idea of a perfect plan because waiting for the perfect plan provides us with the best justification for not taking action. We use the desire for the plan to hide what's really going on behind the scenes.

We're able to justify why we haven't started by telling ourselves and others that, *"We're planning. We're learning. We're getting ready. We're building the foundation."*

I can't tell you how strong of a reaction I have when I hear these excuses. I gag because it's just such a cliché . I just smile and walk away most of the time because I know what's really going on, and I also know that it has nothing to do with what they're saying.

So, what's really going on?

They're scared s***less. That's it. It's pure FEAR.

They're petrified at the idea of potentially failing. As long as we don't start, we won't fail. Boom, the perfect loophole.

Chasing their dreams, taking action, and actually doing something means that they're sticking their necks out. They're officially trying to do something that's innately very difficult. They have to own up to the fact that they may very well **fail.**

Therein lies the problem.

If you never actually start, how will you ever have a chance at success? This is exactly why the *Catapult* stage is so important. This stage is all about getting your start and creating momentum.

It's that momentum that will carry you across the biggest challenges and unknowns of your life, not the *plan.*

Time To Take Action

In this stage, it's time to take action. No more planning. No more trying to make it all perfect. Now it's just about sprinting toward your goal.

You'll fall. You'll take the wrong turns. You'll even get tired.

All of that is ok because it happens to everyone. As long as you're moving forward and focusing on creating momentum, nothing will be able to stop you!

Here are the five factors that we need to uncover to really master the Catapult stage of your journey as an Entrepreneur:

1. **Open Declaration**—This forces us to have accountability.
2. **Focus**—Learning to focus leads to a higher probability of success.
3. **Eating an Elephant**—Breaking down the prospect of taking action into bite-sized pieces.
4. **No More Tomorrow**—Stop putting things off. Take action today! Procrastinating kills the spirit and destroys any chance of success.
5. **Relationship with Failure**—Viewing failure as a good thing, as something to learn from, can tip the scales toward success.

That said, are you ready? Let's do this.

Let's catapult into the next section!

CHAPTER 15:
OPEN DECLARATION

"Remember your dreams and fight for them.
You must know what you want from life."
– Paulo Coelho

I'm an adamant believer in openly declaring my goals.

No matter how scary, daunting, or embarrassing they may be, I will tell anyone and everyone what I dream of achieving.

But I wasn't always this way.

Years ago, my team would hound me about our goals every time we were launching a new product. I would always escape answering their questions by saying, *"I just want to do well."*

However, that response was a lie. Of course I had a specific number in my mind; I just didn't want to tell anyone.

Why?

Because I was afraid.

What if we didn't hit the number? What if we failed? Would I demotivate everyone? Would the team stop trusting me in the future? Would I be embarrassed?

In 2017, I decided to change my tune and try the opposite of what I had been doing. In 2017, we decided to start declaring our monthly revenue targets. Whether they were high or low didn't matter. We agreed as a team to the number and then rallied around it.

The results were simply amazing.

Openly declaring our goals to both the people inside of our company and outside of it created what felt like a *movement*. People rallied. Even third-party partners wanted to get in on the exciting action.

New people appeared. Opportunities opened up. People stretched themselves. All of this happened because we took a minute to say, *"This month we're going to hit ___ in revenue. Period."*

Once that number was declared, I noticed that everyone around us would fight tooth and nail to make it happen.

So, did it work?

Out of the 12 months that we tried it, we hit our goal nine times! What's even crazier is that nobody was embarrassed or demotivated in the three months that we didn't hit our goal. Instead, we rallied and decided to work harder the next month.

Even when we failed, the outcome was good!

But it gets crazier.

As we were openly declaring our goals, we noticed a pattern emerge. Most of those nine months when we hit our numbers, we *just* barely hit our numbers. It often happened on the very last day!

This happened for several months.

Our standard goal for the month was $1.5 million in revenue. On many occasions, we would find ourselves 70% behind our target two or three weeks into the month. Things often didn't look promising.

This is where the open declaration would kick in.

People would start to rally, and we would "magically" cross the $1.5 million goal with just a few hours left in the last day of the month. We would end the month at something like $1,510,000.

Although it became a running joke because it happened so often, the fact that we were able to do it consistently kept people focused, energized, optimistic, and confident even when we were behind on our goal.

Try making an open declaration and you'll see the great power it has.

You'll create support, you'll attract opportunities, you'll find new resources. Most of all, you'll find others who want to help you reach your goals.

You Can't Do This Alone

One of the core lessons of success is that you can't do it alone.

NOBODY can.

If you're not openly sharing your dreams and goals, how is anyone supposed to know? What if the person next to you has the perfect solution to your problem but doesn't even know that you're looking for it?

Ask and you shall receive.

So, why don't more people do it?

Honestly, I can't tell you the goals and dreams of 80% of my friends. I actually texted a few of my friends while I was writing this and asked them for their specific dreams in life. They all gave me some generic answer.

Why is that?

Is it because they don't have a specific dream, or is it because they don't want to share? I'd be willing to put money on the latter. But why not? I'm a close friend to these people. Why wouldn't they tell me?

Do they not trust me? Do they think I'll steal their dream?

Not at all. The reason is actually very simple. **They're scared out of their minds.**

Once they tell me, they're accountable for that dream. It's on the record. What if I remember the dream and ask them about it three years from now? What will they say?

Ironically, that very fear is another reason you should be openly declaring your dreams. The truth is that we could all use a bit more accountability in our lives. If a bit of fear of embarrassment is what it takes to get you off your butt, then why not use it?

The Unexplainable Mysterious Powers

There's an actor who lives in Mumbai, India named Shah Rukh Khan. He was voted by People Magazine as one of the most powerful people in the world—ranking even above Oprah Winfrey.

But he's not just an actor.

You have to think of him as Tom Cruise meets Brad Pitt meets Michael Jordan. Only then do you start to get close to the star power this guy has.

Everyone in India knows who he is. I mean it. Everyone.

Forget knowing who he is, the man is so powerful that thousands of people block the streets in front of his house on certain days of the week just for the small chance that he'll come out and wave to them.

Knowing that, you can imagine how hard it is to meet this man and become friends with him. It's nearly impossible.

Growing up, I had zero interest in Indian movies. I couldn't stand them. I was a *Top Gun, Mission Impossible, James Bond* kind of guy. I don't know what happened, but Bollywood slapped me across the face the day I stepped foot in college.

I started watching Indian movies with my friends on a weekly basis. I would watch these movies and hear all my friends (especially the girls) raving, *"Oh man! Shah Rukh Khan! Shah Rukh Khan! I love him so much!"*

I was intrigued by this man. I decided that I wanted to meet him personally and see for myself why he's such a big deal. It would be a worthwhile challenge.

So I stood up in front of three of my friends and openly declared, "One day, I'm going to be friends with Shah Rukh Khan and others like him. I'm going to have their phone numbers and hang out with them. You just watch and wait."

The first time, my friends just laughed and ignored me. Then for some reason, I started declaring it over and over. It got to the point where some of my friends literally thought I was losing my mind.

I mean, let's look at the facts:

1. I lived in Maryland, USA.
2. I was not an actor.
3. I had zero connection to Mumbai, India.
4. I had no money.
5. I had no family contacts or connections.

At that point, a struggling theatre actor in our small drama school had a better statistical chance of meeting Shah Rukh Khan than I did. However, that didn't stop me from declaring it. I even remember a day when one of my friends (an obsessive fan of Shah Rukh Khan) got very angry at me. She insisted, "Just stop now. It's not funny anymore. Stop talking nonsense."

I was so dumbfounded and confused at her reaction. I was just telling the truth!

Well, time went on and my entire life changed. I left the pre-med track and became a digital Entrepreneur. Just a few years after making that initial declaration, I found myself hiring a freelance developer from Mumbai, India for a small $20 project.

He did a great job, so I gave him more and more work over time. Before I knew it, I was giving him over $10,000 worth of work per month. One thing led to another, and I found myself on a flight to India to meet the entire company.

Long story short, within a couple of years, I bought his company, started my own operation in Mumbai, and began spending almost six months a year there.

Think about that for a minute. Just a few years before I was on track to becoming a doctor with zero reason to even visit Mumbai. Now, here I was living six months out of the year in the same city where Shah Rukh Khan lived. I could have gone to any city in the entire world, but there I was.

As it turned out, Shah Rukh Khan's team was looking for a digital marketing specialist and they heard there was this American guy named Anik Singal who actually had an office in Mumbai. Eventually, they sent a man by the name of Jon Talarico to find me.

Jon not only found me, but today, he's become one of my best friends. Through Jon, I ended up not only meeting Shah Rukh Khan, but I've now been to his home multiple times, offered him advice, and even had the honor of taking a selfie with his world-renowned golden toilet (that's a story for another day).

The bottom line lesson here is that openly declaring your dreams has amazing power behind it and can work in the most strange of ways.

I'm Not The Only One

I am not the only person who uses the power of open declaration.

The biggest and most successful Entrepreneurs in the world are doing it. They often declare things they're going to do YEARS before they do them. I'm talking crazy things. Things that make them sound certifiably insane.

Take Richard Branson, for example.

He came out years ago and said, *"Why do only the astronauts get to go to space? I'm going to build a commercial plane to take people to space, and the first flight will be in 2011.*" Think about that. He wants to take normal folks like you and me to prance around space like it's our backyard. Yep, he's crazy.

Although he missed his goal of flying to space by 2011, does anyone trust him less? No! If anything, he's had time to accrue more support, more resources, more partners, and even more funding. Today, the likelihood of his dream coming true is more solidified than ever before.

And then there's Elon Musk. Here's another "*lunatic.*" He says he's going to build a colony of humans on Mars! It doesn't get any crazier than that, does it? He made this declaration back in 2001 when he didn't even know how to get a rocket made.

Today, he has a line of rockets, successful flights, brilliant engineers, volunteers, and partners rooting him on. He's even raised money from all over the World for the project.

I have absolutely **NO DOUBT** *he will accomplish his goal of colonizing Mars.*

The Power That Open Declaration Gives You

I can go on and on about the power of open declaration, but just know that it's remarkable.

The three powers behind open declaration that make it so impactful are:

1. Accountability
Open declaration makes you ACCOUNTABLE.

Not only to yourself, but to others as well. Once you tell everyone what your dream is, you have to get to work. What will they think of you if you don't?

Although I hate the idea of doing something based on what others think, I can't help but acknowledge that it's a pretty powerful fear. There have been many nights when I've pushed myself an extra few hours because I was thinking about my external accountability to others.

2. Create a Rally

Once people know what you want, they have a chance to help you. Maybe they have a contact for you. Maybe they have a resource for you. Maybe they can help you spread the word. Whatever it is, it only helps.

Many times, declaring your dreams will attract others who share the same dream. This allows you to create a team rather than trying to do everything solo.

3. Focus

When you openly declare what you plan to accomplish, it forces you to think creatively about how you'll make it happen. You become so focused on the goal that it becomes an obsession.

The more you think about it, the more opportunities and options you explore. The more opportunities you explore, the greater your chances are of experiencing success.

Question Time

Now it's time to answer a few questions to see where you stand with open declaration.

Ready?

1. If I asked your best friend what your biggest goal in life is, would he or she be able to give me a specific answer?
2. Would you tell a stranger what your biggest dream is no matter how BIG it is? Even if it makes you sound crazy?
3. How specific is your goal? Can you visualize it? Do you use specifics to describe it, or do you just use generalizations?

For example, I have very specific goals...

"I will unite 1,000,000 Entrepreneurs from all over the world. I will help empower a change in the world through the creation of an army of successful Entrepreneurs. Whether it be world peace, hunger, water or disease, only Entrepreneurs can solve it. Not our governments. So, my mission? I want to provide these Entrepreneurs with every tool they need to be the badasses they already are."

How will I do this?

- #LurnNation will have 1 million members from all over the world by the end of 2019.
- I'll become a self-made billionaire.
- I will help raise one million people out of extreme poverty using the power of Entrepreneurship.

There is no uncertainty or generalization in my goals. I can visualize each of them, and I can openly declare them to anyone without hesitation. I don't care if they think I'm crazy.

All I care about is *my* focus, which also happens to be the subject of our next chapter.

CHAPTER 16:
FOCUS

"People think focus means saying yes to the thing you've got to focus on. But that's not what it means at all. It means saying no to the hundred other good ideas that there are."
– Steve Jobs

Dear Mr. Cuban,

I'm a big fan of yours and what you've achieved. I respect you a lot and would like to have the success that you've had. I'm a young, ambitious college kid and I want to be like you. I'm working on five ideas as an Entrepreneur. I just wanted to know what advice you have for me.

– Anik Singal

This is an email I sent to Mark Cuban back in 2002.

I used to read stories about him all the time in college because I was amazed by who he was and how he had built his fortune. One day, I opened my favorite magazine, Business 2.0 (may it rest in peace), and there was a big article about Mark.

The best part was at the end of the article. In tiny italicized letters, they actually wrote, *"Mark's email address is:_____. If you email him, he'll email you back."*

I remember staring at this claim for an hour thinking, *"Surely this is B.S. Why would a billionaire email me back?"* Finally, I decided I had nothing to lose and fired off an email.

Much to my surprise and excitement, he wrote me back just hours later!

He said, "*Hey kid, got to keep it short. On the way to a game. My advice to you would be to drop four and focus on one.*"

What?

My initial response was one of shock and anger.

I mean, every single successful Entrepreneur I had ever heard of had multiple companies. Even Mark Cuban himself had several companies. *Why was he giving me such outwardly obvious rotten advice?*

I swept that advice under the rug because I thought I knew better than a self-made billionaire. I carried on as I was. A few months later, I went to a seminar in Baltimore and walked into a session called *The Power of Focus.*

Essentially, the topic of the presentation was the same as what Mark had told me. Drop four and focus on just one. The advice was the same, but the way they explained it was very different. This speaker used math in his explanation, so it finally all made sense to me!

The basis of what he said was this.

Say you have 10 projects and each project will take you 100 hours to complete. If you work 10 hours a day, one hour on each project, it would take you 100 days to finish any one of those projects.

If you worked on just one project for 10 hours a day, you would have that project finished in just 10 days. ***10 days!*** Think about how much quicker you could get to market and move if you could be done in 10 days instead 100.

The day I heard this explanation was the day that I went home and deleted four projects from my computer.

I was going to finally focus on just one.

The universe is abundant. Life is abundant. Love is abundant. Time, however, is NOT.

We all only have 24 hours in a day. That's it. No more, no less. No matter who you are, your time is finite. With every hour, every second, let's face it - you're closer to death. These are the laws of physics and we can't change them.

Out of these 24 hours, we have to sleep, we have to run errands, and we have to be with our families. If we assume you'll sleep for just eight hours a day and spend another four hours a day on your other responsibilities – you're left with just 12 hours to put to use towards your dreams.

The question is what to do with those 12 hours.

This is important because **what you focus on is what will get done.** It's as simple as that.

If I focus on nothing but losing weight for the next month, I'll lose weight. But if I'm focused on losing weight, improving my relationship with my wife, and improving my spiritual wellbeing all at the same time, I'll likely get overwhelmed and quit on all three.

Focusing on one thing at a time not only reduces overwhelm, it also increases efficiency.

Getting In The Zone

If you keep switching between different tasks, the quality of your work is going to suffer.

It's all about getting in the zone.

Getting in the zone takes time. Let's go back to the 10 projects at a time example. If you were doing 10 projects at the same time rather than focusing on one at a time, this is what it might look like.

You'll work on each project for one hour a day. So, say you start at 7:00 a.m. You'll work from 7:00 to 7:59 a.m. on the first project. Then you'll work on the second project from 8:00 to 8:59 a.m. Then you'll switch to the third project. This will go on all day until you've worked for 10 hours.

But here's the thing...

You really won't get a solid hour of work in on any of those projects. Why? **Because it takes time to switch mental gears.**

When you sit down to start working on the first project, it'll take you some time to get into a rhythm. You would have to refresh yourself from the work you had previously done to get into the right mindset.

It'll take at least 10 minutes to re-introduce yourself to the project. Then it'll take another five minutes just to get back into the rhythm of that project's work.

That's 15 minutes in and you're finally just getting started.

So it takes 15 minutes just to start, but we're still not in the zone yet.

Think of getting in the zone like trying to push a car parked in neutral. Initially, you'll have to push really hard to get it to move, and you'll probably need more than one person.

However, once that car gets moving, it's got momentum and even just one person, with little to no strength, could walk along the back of the car and gently push it to keep it moving.

To build this kind of momentum with your project, you'll likely need another 10 to 15 minutes. Here you are, 25 to 30 minutes into the project and your engines are finally getting to full throttle.

If you're only allowing yourself one hour, you now have just 30 to 35 minutes of good hard work left until you have to apply the brakes and bring your car halting to a stop again. You lose all your momentum and you have to start the entire process over again for your next project.

Now, imagine if you were focusing on only ONE project at a time? You'll be able to stay in the zone for hours and hours after the initial push.

It's just much more efficient.

Facing The Obstacles

When you're truly focused and committed for the long haul, you're left with no choice but to succeed. That way, you'll be forced to face a daunting obstacle if it steps in your way. You won't have a list of other possible projects to go hide under.

Tony Hsieh, the co-founder of Zappos, is a great example of this.

When he was approached by a young entrepreneur, Nick Swinmurn, about starting an online shoe company, he was intrigued. He decided to take on the project and help build this company.

But the company had a rough start.

The company was struggling and no investors were willing to get involved. So, what did Tony do? He had to make a decision. Was this going to be his main focus? If so, was he willing to give it all he had?

Tony put nearly everything he owned into Zappos. He sold his belongings and invested all the cash into the company.

His family, friends, and business associates all thought he was crazy!

But Tony didn't see it that way.

Tony was committed and focused. He was doing the only logical thing to do at the time. Nothing else mattered. There were no other options for him. It was sink or swim, so he decided he would figure out how to swim.

In the end, Amazon bought Zappos for *$940 million.*

The key lesson here isn't to sell all your assets and invest them into your business. The key lesson is that focus is powerful. Focus allows you to be very clear on your priorities and stay away from distractions.

On the other side, imagine that you're working on 10 projects at the same time and suddenly hit a hard obstacle. What do you think most people will do? They'll drop the project and go work on something else. This may sound good, but this will eventually become a torturous habit that leads to nothing but a cycle of inaction.

Question Time

At this point, I hope you can appreciate how important focus is for an Entrepreneur. Here are a few questions you can answer to find out how focused you are:

1. How many businesses have you modeled out this year?
I call this the Excel trap. If you find yourself coming up with new ideas and modeling them every month, you're not focused.

2. If someone called you right now with a great idea, what would you say? Would you apologize and tell them you don't have the time, or would you start moving things aside to make room for the new project?
Be honest here. Would you just drop everything for a new opportunity or keep your focus on what you're working on at that moment? Would you find yourself easily justifying your decision to take on another project or would you be real with yourself and your time?

3. Are you doing at least one thing daily to become a successful Entrepreneur?
Just think about your current business idea. The one you're focused on right now. Are you doing something every single day to make progress with that business?

How you answer these three questions will give you an idea of how good you are in the area of focus.

Now, for a fun question.

Do you know how to eat an elephant?

CHAPTER 17:
EATING AN ELEPHANT

"The secret of getting ahead is getting started. The secret for getting started is breaking a complex overwhelming task into small manageable tasks, and then starting on the first one."
– Mark Twain

Some of the best advice I ever got was from a drunk man at a bar.

When I was first starting my business, I used to attend a lot of seminars and conferences. But I didn't go to sit in the seminar room to "learn." I would actually go for all the things that would happen after the event was over. My main goal was to be around to network and meet all the guest speakers at the event.

I was in Los Angeles at an event and, after a full day of soaking in the seminars, I decided to retreat to where the real magic happens. I went to the local bar, grabbed a table and ordered some food. Just as planned, the speakers started showing up one after the other, and I couldn't help but spot one particular man in the far corner of the bar.

This man was one of my idols!

He was one of the keynote speakers at the event, someone I had followed very closely for a couple of years. He was too drunk for me to feel comfortable approaching him right away, but a bunch of other speakers from the event started joining him at the bar.

As always, they started talking business.

Their conversation was absolutely stunning because they didn't talk like the rest of us. Their conversation was all about millions of dollars here, millions of dollars there. They were completely casual in their discussion, and here I was struggling to make $10,000 a month.

I was mesmerized and didn't realize that I was staring.

One of them saw me and called me over to join them. I was ecstatic. Here I was getting a chance to hang out with multi-millionaires!

I grabbed my drink, ran over and they immediately gave me a chance to ask my questions. I replied by asking, "How can you all just sit here and so nonchalantly talk about making millions of dollars? I can't even figure out how to make $10,000!"

The drunk man from earlier turned around, looked me right in the eye and said, "Hey, kid. How do you eat an elephant?"

I thought he had lost his mind because I had never heard this analogy before. I just shrugged.

Nearly falling over and chuckling, he said, "One bite at a time." Then he got up and stumbled away into the hallway.

Focus On What Comes Next

Sitting there that evening, I thought I understood what he meant and the other speakers confirmed it for me.

"Don't think about the millions. Think about what you need to do next. Your next goal is to hit $10,000. Focus on that. Once you've hit $10,000, then focus on hitting $100,000 - just do what you did to make $10,000, 10 times."

I realized right then and there that this is *exactly* how I had started making money on the internet in the first place. Yet here I was stressing over creating a plan to make a million dollars when I hadn't even made $10,000.

I was putting the cart before the horse.

I remember the day I made my first $300 with my online business.

I knew if I could just make $300 every day, I would be earning $109,500 a year. I couldn't believe that while sitting in college, still technically unsure what I wanted to do with my life, I could be earning a *six-figure salary*.

But the focus wasn't on $100,000. The focus was on $300 a day.

As my business grew, I made a bet with my friend about who could make $2,000 in a week first. I hadn't realized it, but I was changing my goal from $300 to focus on $2,000 – taking a step up. Here I was, eating an elephant one bite at a time and I never even realized it.

The only thing that the winner would get would be bragging rights. Just having an open declaration of the goal made us both hustle harder for it. Well, I got energized with creativity and made $2,000 in just a few days!

But that was where I stopped, and that was my biggest mistake. I should have announced a second goal of $5,000 or any number marginally higher than $2,000. I should have kept eating the elephant one bite at a time. However, I went straight from $2,000 to wanting to make millions.

I didn't realize it then, but that jump was way too big for my mind. It didn't necessarily inspire me as much as it demotivated and frightened me.

The drunk man made me realize that I needed to think about my goals differently, and he damn well changed my life!

Changed My Thinking

Those millionaires helped me change my whole way of thinking. I decided to take everything one step at a time.

After that night at the bar, I decided to stop focusing on the millions and put my focus on $10,000. I couldn't believe it, but just that small shift led me to earning $10,000 in the next two weeks.

Before that night, I had been stalled for two months. I was struggling to grow and my income wasn't consistent until that day. Suddenly, the smaller goal made me more creative and helped me seek more opportunities. Before I knew it, I was back to growing!

Since that day, I've come to realize that so many people are worried about things that don't make any sense, about things that don't actually exist.

For example, what did I learn from those guys about making a million dollars? First, you make $100. That's it. Just $100. Then take what you did to make that $100 and do it 10 times. You'll have made $1,000. Then take what you did to make $1,000 and do that 10 times, and you'll have made $10,000. Then take what you did to make $10,000, do it 10 times, and you'll have made your first $100,000. Finally, take what you did to make $100,000, do it 10 times, and you'll have made your first $1 million.

I realize how simplistic this sounds, but that's the beauty of it. It really can be this simple!

We're the ones that complicate things that don't need to be complicated.

Driving To Toronto

I was at a Bob Proctor seminar doing my rounds and talking to all the attendees. I started realizing a major theme among many of the students there. Everyone seemed so worried about the *how*.

- *How* will I start my own business?
- *How* will I earn my first million dollars?
- *How* will I find the right team?
- *How* will I get the support of my family?

As the attendees spoke to me, that was all they wanted. They wanted my *how*. The problem is that my *how* is very unique to me. I doubt that anyone could have copied my exact process. I found myself telling everyone that the *how* is not important. Instead, focus more on the *what*.

Well, that wasn't making sense to anyone either.

To make matters worse, Bob suddenly called upon me and asked me to come speak on stage. Well, the only thing on my heart at that moment was this topic of *how*.

I needed to figure out a way to explain this to everyone when suddenly it hit me.

I asked the audience if anyone there knew exactly how to drive from Washington, D.C. to Toronto, Canada. Everyone gave me a dumbfounded look. No one knew. I told them that I didn't either. However, I wouldn't even break a sweat if I needed to make the drive.

Why?

Because I would just type the address into my navigation and start following the instructions. The car would say turn left and I would. The car would say go straight for two miles and I would. I could even make a wrong turn and the car would automatically reroute me to correct for my mistake.

The key is that I would never be worried about *how*. I would only be worried about the *what*. Suddenly, I could see the students in the audience starting to light up. One even yelled, "Oh man, that's brilliant!"

Then I laid the final punch to my point.

"Let's say you put an address into your navigation. Would you be worried about what turns you're going to take 20 turns from now? Would you ask the navigation to tell you about what you'll be doing in two hours? Of course not!"

Why do we spend so much of our time worrying about bridges that we're not even ready to cross yet? Why not just focus on the short-term and trust the process along the way? Even if we make a wrong turn, our life will pivot to correct for it.

We'll never have an exact *how* – everyone will be different and part of the journey will be for us to discover our own path.

Micro-Steps

When we have goals in life, we tend to focus on the biggest one. We stare at it and focus on what we need to do 20 or 30 turns ahead of where we are. *When we do this, we're focusing on the completely wrong things.*

The secret to reaching a goal is actually focusing on the micro-steps along the way. We have to focus on creating small win after small win. If we stare only at the big end goal, it's simply too overwhelming.

Think of it this way, the road to success is not an elevator or an escalator. It's a stairwell that you have to take one step at a time.

The first thing I recommend you do is take your big goal and break it down into smaller goals. Start to focus on the one right in front of you and put yourself squarely on the journey toward your end goal. This one trick alone is probably responsible for a large majority of my success.

Join Forces With Your Mind

Affirmations are a big deal, right?

So many people promote them. Just keep saying the same thing to yourself over and over again and your mind will eventually believe it.

I hate to say it, but I don't believe this at all. Before many people cry bloody murder, let me tell you why.

Let's say I looked at myself in the mirror right now and I told myself, "I'm a billionaire. I'm a billionaire. I'm a billionaire." Every single time I said that to myself, my mind would say, *"HA! No, you're not. No, you're not. No, you're not."*

Instead of trying to trick my mind into believing something that might be too much for it to take in, why not join forces with my mind? If my mind is not willing to accept that I'm a billionaire, then maybe I should stop telling it that.

Here's what I mean.

If I currently earn $1 million a year, telling my mind that we're going to earn $100 million a year may be too big of a leap for my mind. It may be too much of a stretch and my mind may subconsciously start to work against me. However, my mind would be absolutely fine hearing me say, *"I'm going to make $5 million a year or $10 million a year."*

This is still a stretch, but it's a stretch that my mind doesn't immediately throw out. In time, as you train your mind to accept bigger goals, you'll see that it's willing to accept larger statements. But when you're starting out...

Eat your goals like you would an elephant!

Question Time

To see how strong you are already on what we've discussed above, I want you to answer these questions with the first thought that comes to your mind.

1. What's the first micro-goal you have? Can you answer super fast?
You have to be able to answer this question fast. If you didn't answer it fast, you're not currently eating an elephant one bite at a time.

2. When you serve yourself food, do you tend to go for a huge plate up front, or do you like to go for less food and do more trips?
I know this seems like a silly question, but it says a lot about how you look at tackling goals and life. I actually noticed this about myself and have since changed the way I visit the buffet lines!

3. Do you spend more time asking questions about what to do <u>today</u>, or do you get lost in questions that are related to the future?
I love looking far ahead. After all, I'm the one who said I want to be a self-made billionaire. But first make sure that you have today covered. Do you

know exactly what steps you need to take today to make your goals happen?

Speaking about *today*, it's time to discuss my next mantra, *no more tomorrow*.

CHAPTER 18:
NO MORE TOMORROW

"Leave nothing for tomorrow which can be today."
– Abraham Lincoln

"Anik, you can't just start a business! You have to get experience and learn first."

This is what I was told repeatedly during my first year of college when I was trying to start my own business. I was out there openly declaring my intention to start a business and all I was getting back from everyone was this nonsense about "experience."

Honestly, it made absolutely no sense to me.

Why couldn't I just learn by doing? I was dumbfounded by the idea that I had to sit through years of classes to start my own business when everything I needed was right in front of me.

Fortunately, I didn't take the bad advice. Very early on, I caught a trend among those who were the most vocal.

They weren't Entrepreneurs!

What made them credible enough to give me any advice on the subject? That's like an engineer trying to tell a doctor how to do surgery. It's literally that absurd.

So I ignored all the "get experience" advice and decided to throw myself in. I had faith in myself. I knew that I could figure it out if I applied myself. I hadn't failed at anything yet in my life, and I most certainly wasn't going to start now.

Essentially, I decided to start becoming an Entrepreneur immediately instead of waiting until the day when someone else gave me permission.

There's a bad trait of which we're all guilty.

Ready?

I'll do it tomorrow.

Every day we get up and give ourselves a list of all the things we'll do. As the day goes on, we let ourselves get distracted and pulled in many directions.

Eventually, we end up missing out on the most important dream building tasks and instead resort to, "*I'll wait until tomorrow when I have more time.*" However, we never let ourselves believe that it was our fault or that we failed at keeping our word.

We find all kinds of excuses and justifications for putting something off until tomorrow.

We say…

- Let me learn more and then I'll do it better.
- I still need to do my research.
- I'll be more focused tomorrow.
- I'll have more time to do a stellar job tomorrow.
- ____ is visiting tomorrow and they're going to be an amazing help on this task!

The list of justifications and excuses could literally go on and on, but here's the real reason why people put things off.

They're afraid of failing and don't want to face that reality.

Rather than being honest and admitting that to themselves, they find justification after justification to keep putting things off.

The worst part is that this becomes a cycle.

There are people who have gone months, if not years, playing the tomorrow game. It's crazy. Take a minute and think about this.

Let's assume you promise yourself that you'll start something on Monday, but when Monday comes you delay it to Tuesday. When Tuesday comes, you delay it to Wednesday, and so on and so on.

What do you think is happening over time the more you do this?

Losing Trust In Yourself

Think of it this way.

Say you had a friend you were supposed to meet for lunch at noon on Monday. You show up at the restaurant, get a table, and wait. A half an hour passes. Then an hour. But your friend is still nowhere to be seen.

Finally, you get a phone call and your friend says, "I'm so sorry. I couldn't make it out of work. I really owe you. I will be there tomorrow at 12:00. I'll even be there early. I'm so sorry."

You say, "Yeah, no problem. It happens."

But when the next day comes and you show up at noon, your friend isn't there. Again, you wait and he doesn't show. Again, he calls and apologizes, "I am so sorry again! We're on for tomorrow and lunch is on me. I owe you. I promise I'll be there."

Wednesday comes along and you show up at the restaurant at noon. You wait and wait and AGAIN your friend doesn't show.

Now, let me ask you this—*how many times will you put up with this before you say forget it?*

How many times does your friend have to ditch you before you lose faith in him or her? Probably not many. That third time being stood up was probably your last.

Yet we stand ourselves up on a daily basis. We are constantly defeating ourselves on a subconscious level. Every single time we don't follow through, we lose faith in ourselves and in our ability to make our dreams come true.

Do It Today

Eliminate tomorrow completely!

There's no such thing as tomorrow. It doesn't exist as anything more than a date on the calendar. You MUST face the challenges, the obstacles, and the chance of failure TODAY.

Do whatever you need to do, but get that one thing you've been dragging on done today. If that means you don't sleep tonight, fine. If that means you skip dinner, fine. If that means you have to cancel big plans with someone, so be it.

Put your dreams first – whatever that one thing is, make a declaration and don't go to sleep today without having it finished, period.

My Pet Peeve

You know, one of my biggest pet peeves is when the people I work with, whether it be students or my team members, say to me, "Great idea, Anik. I'll do it tomorrow." Or, "What a great idea, I'll send them an email."

I really can't stand this. Why wait until tomorrow? Why not today? Why send an email? Get in front of that person and get an answer now! Where's the urgency? Why are we so complacent to sit around and wait for things to happen? I got to where I am by always commanding someone's attention, by always doing what was needed at that very moment.

How often do *you* do that? How often do you hear about something, get excited, send someone an email and then sit back and wait for that person to get back to you? Your actions, your dreams, your everything is waiting on *someone else* to make it possible.

Imagine how many much is wrong with that picture!

When you do this, you are literally giving FULL control of the success of your project to someone else. You are sitting around waiting for permission to move forward and succeed.

Do you really want to do this?

The whole point of this chapter is urgency, and I remind my team of this all the time. Entrepreneurs are impatient people. They will not wait until tomorrow—they will do whatever they need to do to get it done today.

Bill Gates' BASIC Leap

Bill Gates understood the need to take action today.

In fact, he and his partner, Paul Allen, both understood the urgency of seizing the day so much so that they promised something they hadn't even created yet.

When Bill Gates was in college, he and Paul Allen would ditch classes to work in the computer room at school. They had managed to create a program that earned them $20,000. Later that year, they saw an article about the first microcomputer, the Altair 8800. Bill and Paul immediately seized the day and called the company to tell them that they had written a version of the BASIC computer language for the Altair computer.

Here's the crazy thing.

They hadn't written a single line of code yet. They were just saying what they needed to say to get the door open!

Well, the door swung open wide.

After that, they spent day and night in Harvard's computer lab developing the actual code that they had promised. Just in the nick of time, they finished it all and got it done. The craziest part is that when they flew all the way to Altair, they didn't have a clue if the code would even work.

Whether they had something or not, the important thing is that they never waited for someone else. They didn't fire off an email and sit around twiddling their thumbs. No, they went out and grabbed the day by the horns!

So, back to my original challenge for you.

I can virtually guarantee you're sitting on something you've been planning on doing for a long time, but it keeps getting pushed back. I challenge you to go out and do it today, or at least get a start – no more tomorrow!

Be Execution Minded

Listen, I know we talked about how important studying, reading, and educating yourself is. I still stand by that, but I don't want you to use it as a crutch either. If you're using your studying as a way to make excuses for not taking action, then you're truly hurting yourself.

Entrepreneurs are execution specialists. The best ones don't know where, how, when, or what. They just start running and commit to figuring it out as they go. So, yes, make sure you study, but more than that, make sure you're sticking your neck out daily and taking action.

Entrepreneurs do NOT sit around waiting for anything.

Question Time

With this in mind, here are some questions for you to answer:

1. If you have a work question, do you use some form of instant messaging for an answer or do you email them?
How immediate do you make your communication? How direct? Do you approach it in such a way that you get your question answered when YOU want it answered, or do you have to put off your work until you get an answer?

2. How often do you find yourself saying, "It's okay. I'm tired today. I'll definitely do this tomorrow!"
Be honest. How often do you do this? If it's more than once in a while, then you have a problem.

3. Do you ask a lot of questions when asked to do something?
Are you the type of person that, when asked to do something, will respond with 32 questions? Are you the person who makes sure they have as much information as possible up front?

I know that sounds great, but believe it or not, that's usually NOT an Entrepreneur's way. That's typically the way of someone with an employee mindset. Entrepreneurs get going right away, and ask their questions as they go along.

Consider that the main reason so many people keep pushing their dreams off to tomorrow is the FEAR they live with.

The fear of failure.

Let's dive into the relationship YOU have with failure.

CHAPTER 19:
RELATIONSHIP WITH FAILURE

"Without failure there is no achievement."
– John C. Maxwell

It was THE biggest product launch of my career. I had worked on it for months over many sleepless nights. All of our promoters were ready to go. All of our sales pages were ready to go.

Our product was AMAZING.

This one launch was about to change the entire trajectory of my company.

Then, within 7 minutes of going live, EVERYTHING came crashing down.

My servers crashed so bad that we couldn't even reboot them. My technical team had prepared for everything except one thing – the server load. This meant that the thousands of people who had been waiting for and anticipating our product for weeks were now clicking to our page and landing on a dead page. Nothing. Nada.

One by one, my email, my phone, my Skype – everything started to blow up. From customers to our top promoters, everyone was livid. Customers had spent hours waiting by their computers for our launch, and promoters had nothing to show for the weeks they had invested into hyping up the launch.

To say that I was panicked would be a great understatement. I was close to having a total mental breakdown, but the adrenaline of trying to fix the problem kept me running. I had to take a step back and actively make a decision. Was I going to freak out and quit, or was I going to find a way out of this mess?

Honestly, it didn't look good.

Many people in that situation would just throw in the towel, wait for the servers to start working again, and then let whatever sales they could get come in. But I didn't want just "any sales." I wanted the launch event that would change the future of my company.

I chose to get over my panic. I was going to figure out how to save this launch and make it just as big as I had planned. Now, I never said it was going to be easy. I even knew that saving this launch would be a grand feat, but that's why I'm an Entrepreneur, right?

That decision to fight led me to do something I've never tried again and hopefully never will have to. I sat in my office working, without a single minute of sleep, for a total of 56 hours straight. I had clothes brought to me. I had food brought to me. I refused to step out of my office. I took the reins and started studying servers myself. I called in all my contacts who knew more than me and put my network to use. Within that 56-hour window, I figured out what the problem was and how to solve it.

I got on the phone and called each and every one of our promoters to apologize and tell them how I would make it up to them. Basically, I planned to let the launch fizzle out and then relaunch it in 36 hours. After ample server testing, I would send out emails and re-create that spike of interest.

The result?

We went on to have exactly what I had dreamt of. That product launch took off like a soaring eagle and put my company on a different road.

That launch could have been the worst launch of my life. However, with just a little re-positioning in my mind, I turned it into the biggest product launch I had done at that point in my career.

All I did was look at the "failure" through a different lens.

That's it!

You see, what I did when the launch failed was what I do every time something bad happens to me – *I looked for a silver lining.*

My biggest goal became to learn from the failure, the pain, and the hurt. I knew that if I could go the rest of my life without making that same mistake again I'd be much better off. I knew that I might even be thankful for the small failure I had!

Did you read that? Thankful!

I've learned to not only accept failure, but to appreciate it and be grateful for it. The greatest of Entrepreneurs fail on a daily basis. We learn more from our failures than we'll ever learn from our successes. Specifically, I celebrate my failure because I know that, statistically speaking, every failure brings me closer to success.

Hence, every time I fail I learn a new way NOT to do something. I think it's a huge win and a lifelong lesson.

Thankful For Falling $1.7 Million in Debt

Think about this. When I fell $1.7 million in debt, my life was hanging by a thread. My dad had mortgaged his home for me. My friends had emptied their bank accounts for me. I was close to being sued by banks. My health was falling apart. Seriously, it was like a scene from a movie.

Can you imagine me coming out of that entire situation and being grateful for it?

I actually thank God every day that I experienced that catastrophe early in my career so that I could learn from it. That entire three-year period of falling into great debt and climbing back out of it taught me:

- Mistakes never to make again.
- My strengths and my weaknesses.

- How resilient I am.
- How amazing my family is.
- How blessed I am to have friends who will risk their lives for me.
- What role ego can play in one's life.
- To never, ever give up.

I could go on forever.

You can't learn these lessons in school or in any training program. If I hadn't learned them years ago, I'd have to learn them some other time in my career. Who knows, maybe by then I'd have hundreds more employees, a family of my own, and thousands more customers.

The damage of learning these lessons later in my career could have been catastrophic. That's why I'm thankful that I learned this lesson when I did.

I'm thankful that I failed so bad.

That very failure has helped shape me into the man I am today.

My 3-Year-Old Nephew Got It

Over the years, I've come to realize that mastering a relationship with failure is NOT just about growing in business. It can be applied to any facet of your life. It's such a simple concept that even when my nephew was three-year-old, he could understand it.

One day, I was with my nephew and my sister. My nephew was running all around the house and jumping up and down on the couch. I kept telling him to stop, but he wouldn't listen. The next thing I knew, he tripped and went flying off the couch, landing three feet away with a big THUMP sound. Oh, it sounded painful. Sure enough, seconds later he was crying like he had never cried before.

I picked him up, looked him right in the face and asked him one simple question, "Now, what did you learn?"

As soon I asked the question, my sister started laughing at me saying, "He's three!"

I said, "No, it's okay. He's capable of processing this. What did you learn?" He kept on sobbing and wouldn't answer me, but I wouldn't let up, "I'm sorry, but I won't let you go until you tell me what you learned."

Finally, there it was. He stopped crying, wiped his tears away and said, "I learned not to jump on the couch."

I said, "Great. For the rest of your life, you'll never have to worry about getting hurt by jumping on the couch and falling off." This short bit of pain he went through was pain well invested for a future of never having to deal with it again.

Mistakes Are Great

Mistakes are absolutely great as long as you NEVER make the same mistake twice.

In other words, it's new mistakes that are awesome. Duplicated or repeated mistakes are stupid. The key is to learn from your mistakes and failures so that you don't repeat them. That's the only way to march toward success.

Always be looking for your silver lining!

Any mistake you make will be a waste unless you can immediately pin down the lesson you learned from it. You need to make sure that you know exactly what went wrong and how you plan to never make that mistake again.

As long as you have a silver lining and a commitment to never making the same mistake twice, I'm telling you now – failure will be your greatest friend, teacher, and asset.

Now, it's time for you to answer a few questions:

1. Are you afraid of hearing a NO?
Most people are, but here's what you need to know. Even the most successful people hear the word no all the time. Hearing a no is basically a mini-failure. It's a great chance to learn, pivot and re-attack.

In sales, the top salesman is always the one who can hear no and never let that be the end. They don't give up on a no. They just regroup and attack again.

So, what do you do when you hear a no?

2. If I asked you when was the last time you truly failed, how long ago would it be?
Can you think of something off the top of your head? If you can, this means that you're paying attention to your failures on some level. For me, I had an epic failure just two days before writing this.

It was embarrassing. I was very upset with myself. I let myself sulk about it for two hours. Then got up, got my journal out, and started writing down what I had learned. By the time I was done, I knew exactly why I had failed. Actually, I was shocked I hadn't failed even more miserably!

But, lesson learned.

Before that failure, it would have been just three days prior to the last one. That means two memorable failures in just a week. Believe it or not, that's actually a really good week for me.

As you can tell, I love failing. I fail often, I fail fast, and I fail forward.

3. When you do fail, is your first thought negative or is it optimistic?
This is so important. Being angry, frustrated, sad, or upset is normal after a failure. These are normal human feelings and we should all be allowed to feel them.

Just like I said above, the last failure I had was pretty big. I spent two hours stewing in my room. I felt jealousy, anger, embarrassment, disappointment, rage – you name it. Here's where the difference was. I let myself feel that way for about two hours before putting an end to it.

I turned those negative feelings into positive learning experiences. I walked away from it all feeling very hopeful about the future. I was just imagining how well I'd perform the next time with all this knowledge under my belt!

See that? I left the failure feeling hopeful.

It's weird to say, but you need a very positive and hopeful relationship with failure. Get that down and you're going to see great success because of it.

With that, we've now taken a good long look at how to master Stage #2 of your eSCAPE plan, Catapult. You've learned...

1. How to make an open declaration.
2. The importance of focus.
3. Taking things one small step at a time.
4. Never waiting for tomorrow.
5. How to appreciate and learn from failure.

Now, it's time to take what you've learned and move on to the next stage of your Entrepreneurial journey. It's time to learn how to have **Authority** and become a leader – an absolutely necessary skill for any successful Entrepreneur.

STAGE 3: AUTHORITY (A)

CHAPTER 20:
A – AUTHORITY

"The greatest leader is not necessarily the one who does the greatest things.
He is the one that gets the people to do the greatest things."
– Ronald Reagan

In my junior year of high school, I was a leader on so many levels.

Even though I wasn't technically an Entrepreneur at this point in my life, I was the leader of four different clubs, including…

- President of the Student Government
- President of the National Honor Society
- President of the Finance Club
- Vice President of our Culture Association

As if that weren't enough, I was also leading my entire high school with the most volunteer hours clocked at the local hospital – I had over 300 hours of volunteer service. I also had a 4.0 GPA.

Needless to say, I was on the go at all times. Any chance I got to lead, I always stepped up. When I look back, I can see this trend of "stepping up to lead" going as far back as fourth grade. Even then, I was always the class leader.

In other words, I've had practice in being a leader ever since I was a child, a talent that has truly paid dividends for me as an Entrepreneur.

However, for every time I was leading, there were countless kids who were not. Think about it. In a group, you only have one leader. So, growing up, the odds of us getting appropriate exposure to leadership are slim to none.

But it's never too late.

Follow the guidelines we provide in this stage and you can brush up on your leadership skills fast.

Becoming A Leader

Even the idea of learning leadership tends to make most people very anxious (and understandably so). In fact, the systems in which we are raised have unknowingly trained us to become followers from the time we're children.

Leadership is a very uncomfortable concept for many because we get no introduction to it as we grow up – at least not everyone. Only the students who really choose to stick their necks out get the exposure, but then those kids end up hogging all the opportunities. I bet as far back as you can remember, you've had parents, teachers, coaches and bosses available at a moment's notice. Essentially, you're accountable to them, not yourself. You always have someone breathing down on you, so your entire motivation for completing tasks is different.

This means we have years of programming built into us. It will definitely take some time, but we can write new code over it. Just be ready to have an open mind.

Is Leadership Mandatory?

I'm going to be honest with you...

The *Authority* stage might just be *the* most challenging of all the stages.

You're going to need to make CORE changes to your way of thinking, and this will definitely take time and dedication. Leadership and authority aren't easy and require learning a lot of frustrating lessons – there's no shortcut.

However, I do have good news for you.

If you're too anxious to lead, or if you determine after some practice that it's just not your thing, there is a solution that allows you to become an

Entrepreneur without having to lead. In Stage #4, we're going to talk about People – this means we're going to talk about team building.

You'll learn how you can plug the holes of your weakness by bringing in the appropriate talent or partnering with the right people.

You do NOT have to master the eSCAPE formula perfectly. Please know that. There isn't a single Entrepreneur who's perfect. We all have our own weaknesses and most of the greatest success stories are full of flaws.

Our goal is to simply master as many of these traits as possible, and become self-aware of the traits we can't master so that we can plug those holes.

However, don't take this and run now. I still want you to learn and hone as much of your leadership and authority as you can.

The Key Elements To Leadership

There are five key elements to developing Authority and leadership that we're going to cover in this stage:

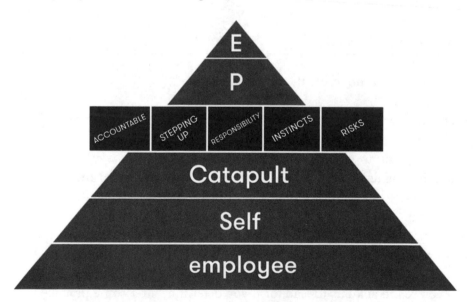

1. Accountability to Self vs. Boss
2. Stepping Up to Lead, Not Follow
3. Taking Responsibility, Not Scapegoating
4. Developing Instincts
5. Taking Calculated Risks

So, let's dive right into Stage #3 by talking about your accountability.

To whom are you truly accountable? Your boss or yourself?

CHAPTER 21:
ACCOUNTABILITY TO SELF VS. BOSS

"Accountability is the measure of a leader's height."
– Jeffrey Benjamin

One morning, a few years ago, I was stuck in morning rush hour traffic on the highway. As I was sitting there, I looked at the car next to me and this is what I saw...

A guy with a bagel in one hand and an electric razor in the other. He was driving with his knees while using the rear-view mirror to help him get the perfect shave.

I was dumbfounded! I felt like he should be featured on America's Got Talent. I remember chuckling to myself as I thought, *"This guy probably woke up late and is in a panic because he's accountable to his boss."* He was accountable to being at work by a certain time. If he was late, he was going to get into trouble. There could be no better example of forced accountability.

Something tells me he didn't choose to be in a situation where he'd be driving with his knees while shaving using his rear-view mirror. This man felt so accountable to his boss that he was going to make it to work on time no matter what he had to do.

While watching this scene play out in front of me, I couldn't help but think about Entrepreneurs. We don't have bosses, so do we have that level of accountability to ourselves?

The painful truth for the majority of the population is a resounding no.

Hitting The Snooze Button

I like to wake up at 7:00 a.m. every day, which is early compared to where I was just a couple of years ago. My rule for waking up early every day is that I'm not allowed to hit the snooze button more than once.

If I hit it more than once, I am NOT being accountable to myself.

This is a very simple exercise in building self-accountability, but it's an important one. It's the first place you start your day and also the easiest place to let things slide.

It's really easy to justify sleeping in, especially when you're your own boss. However, that behavior is exactly what we're trying to avoid because it sets up a precedent for all of the other areas in your life.

Self-accountability is all about building and shaping the trust that we have with ourselves. If we don't trust ourselves, what else could possibly make up for that?

Be Hard On Yourself

Entrepreneurs tend to be harder on themselves than most other people and bosses ever could be. They work longer hours than their employed counterparts, and they push themselves further than most of their peers. However, this doesn't have to be a bad thing.

We push ourselves harder because we prioritize our dreams. We push ourselves harder because we want more than our peers want. The best gift of pushing ourselves harder is that it builds and reinforces our self-accountability.

The harder we push, the more confidence we build in ourselves. When we follow through on that end, we learn to trust ourselves.

Now, this habit of higher self-expectation doesn't just apply to an Entrepreneur's professional life. It usually carries over to their personal lives as well. When I was in college, I had two very significant things happen to me, and both of them caused me to push harder than ever before.

The first thing was that I got very sick and had to go through a series of surgeries in the first semester of my second year of college. This meant that I had to pull out of the first semester of college in each of my first two years of college. I essentially missed an entire year of credits, which meant that I was likely to graduate a year later than everyone else.

To make matters worse, I decided to switch my major from medicine to business in my junior year. Because of that, I fell even further behind on my prerequisite courses. All in all, my counselors estimated that I was at least a year and a half behind on my studies. Maybe even two years.

Needless to say, I wasn't prepared to accept that. There was no way I was going to watch all my childhood friends graduate while I sat on the sidelines. So, I decided to set the record straight. I decided to show the world just who Anik Singal was.

I decided to bunker down and find a path to graduating on time.

I took an extra load of classes during the normal semester and gave up my winter and summer breaks to load up on the maximum amount of credits my university would allow. I even started attending a local community college on the side to get more class credits in.

I had to do this for two years, but I had promised myself that I would graduate on time. There was no way I was going to let myself down.

Guess what? I did it! I graduated with everyone else in my class.

But here's the thing.

In the grand scheme of things, hustling so hard to finish on time wasn't really that necessary. Even if I had taken an extra year to get my degree, it really wouldn't have mattered much. But that wasn't the point.

The point was that I wanted to challenge myself and see myself conquer a goal. It's times like these that have built my self-confidence, and those lessons have carried over into my Entrepreneurial ventures. I've been through so much that I truly believe impossible is only an opinion.

This level of faith and belief is the result of years of trust building and confidence boosting.

Not having self-accountability is a very slippery slope.

Think of it this way.

If an employee is 10 minutes late and the boss lets it go two or three times, what happens? For most people, that 10 minutes will become 15 minutes. If the boss lets that slide too, it'll soon become 20 minutes. It will continue to get worse and worse until someone finally gets in trouble.

In other words, people end up sliding down the wrong slope when they aren't held accountable for their actions.

I think you can see now why things are run so tight in most workplaces. It's unfortunate, but most of us are never really taught to be self-accountable. The minute we lose the authority figure in our lives, we're not equipped with the skills to stay on the right path.

You're either accountable or you're not.

This is exactly why you have very little wiggle room on self-accountability. From something as small as hitting the snooze button to something as big as coming through on your promise to yourself to launch a business – you just don't have any room for compromise.

There's an old saying that goes, *"The way you do one thing is how you do everything."* Just think about that – if you let yourself slide in self-accountability in a seemingly small area, it's going to quickly bleed over into other areas of your life as well.

So, make a commitment to never let yourself down. If you said you'll do something, hold yourself accountable and make sure you do it just like you said you would.

Here's an entirely new view on accountability as it relates to being a leader. How on earth do you think you can you expect your team to be accountable if you aren't? How can you demand certain standards from them when you aren't willing to work to those same standards?

It's simple. You can't.

Leadership starts at the top. You have to lead by example. If you constantly miss your deadlines or go back on your word – you better be prepared to get the same behavior back from your team. So, it's your decision.

As an Entrepreneur, we have to be demanding of our team. Most small companies are usually trying to do three times as much with a third of the staff, so everyone has to hustle harder and hold themselves to much higher standards. With the need to be so demanding of your team, accountability becomes a big topic of discussion.

In fact, Elon Musk and Steve Jobs have both been known for being horrible to their employees. They've been known to make people work for 80 or more hours in a week, many times not even letting them go home at night.

Well, these Entrepreneurs were trying to change the world. At some level, they felt that they had no choice but to demand a lot from their employees. They needed soldiers committed to their cause, so they pushed like all hell.

But here's the thing to remember...

Both of these Entrepreneurs might have been hated by some of their team members, but not a single one of those team members didn't respect them.

Why?

Because if Elon Musk asked his team to stay all night, he would always be right there next to them getting his hands dirty. If you want to have accountability from your team, you need to build the habit of being accountable to yourself.

Remember, people are *always* watching.

Question Time

With all of this in mind, it's time to ask yourself some tough questions.

1. If you were very close to a deadline and your client said, "Don't worry about it. Send it to me tomorrow." What would you do?
Do you push to finish it or put it off?

Be honest here. What would you do?

2. Do you miss deadlines consistently?
I want you to really think about this. When you set your own work schedule, do you stick with it?

I'm guilty of this, and I'm working on it every single day. Even though I find myself very accountable, I still have areas I can work on and improve!

3. How many times do you hit the snooze button?
Do you get right up or press it once, twice, three times? More?

The combination of the answers you give here will give you an idea of how accountable you are to yourself. Then you'll be able to decide if this is an area you need to work on or not. Again, it's okay if you fail this part – most people do. The idea is to learn what you need to improve.

So, start thinking more about self-accountability. Meditate on it. Live it daily. Just being conscious of it will make you much better at it.

For now, it's time for us to move on to the next step, "Stepping Up To Lead…"

CHAPTER 22:
STEPPING UP TO LEAD, NOT FOLLOW

"The ultimate measure of a man is not where he stands in moments of comfort, but where he stands at times of challenge and controversy."
– Martin Luther King Jr.

Have you ever watched kids in a classroom when a teacher asks a question?

When I was a kid, I noticed that my classmates exhibited some strange behavior when this would happen. In the fifth grade, I remember seeing my classmates watching the teacher as she wrote on the blackboard. As she had us flip through our books, they kept straight eye contact. Then, every time she turned around and asked a question, the kids would immediately look away.

They would look around the room or act like they were writing - anything to avoid eye contact with the teacher.

Now, the challenge was that I definitely wasn't one of these kids.

My hand would shoot into the sky even if I wasn't 100% sure that I knew the answer. It didn't matter what the teacher needed. Whether she was asking a simple question or looking for a volunteer, I liked to step up.

Yet, the fact that no one else would do the same started to bother me. What bothered me the most was that even the smartest kids in the class (who I was 100% sure knew the answer) would never volunteer. It completely mystified me.

So, one day I finally snapped and asked my teacher, "Why do the other kids look away when you ask questions? Why don't they raise their hands?"

I'll never forget her answer. She said, "They're afraid that I'll call on them if I see them, and they'll feel humiliated if they get the answer wrong."

I still remember my protest to this day.

#1 - The smartest kids know the answer. What exactly is the risk?

#2 - Even if they are wrong, what's the big deal? No one's going to care or even remember 15 minutes later!

I looked right at my teacher and made my arguments. Other than a small chuckle, she offered me no satisfactory answer. However, I spent days thinking about that encounter. I remember being so confused by it.

Even at that young age, the concept of leadership was brewing inside of me.

I could do it because I didn't innately have this fear of being wrong or being called out. It allowed me to step up when others wouldn't.

Leadership Is Stepping Up

That is exactly what leadership is – *stepping up when the opportunity presents itself.*

Some people are born with a natural inclination to lead while others have to learn it as they go. However, growing up in our educational system gives those who need to learn leadership an unfortunate start.

See, the kids who are eager to lead hog all the opportunities. They raise their hands first every time. They step up to volunteer first every time. They quickly become class leaders, group captains, and student government candidates.

And that's the problem…

Our System Doesn't Teach Leadership

There's no class in school that teaches leadership.

Very few of us ever even get the opportunity to lead. Think about it. There are so many students in a school, yet so few leadership opportunities. You might have 40 students in a class, but there's usually only one class leader. A sports team may have upwards of 60 kids on the team, but there's usually only one team captain.

The worst part of it all is that we, as a society, accept this. We allow for only a few students to experience leadership. We accept it when kids step back because they're hesitant to lead. Rather than teach those kids how to lead, we find it easier to let the "usual" leaders step back up to the plate.

We don't coach, guide, teach, or help them get used to stepping up. In doing this, we're depriving ourselves of entire generations of amazing leaders.

Leadership Is A Skill

Yes, leadership can be learned. It's a skill that CAN be built and nurtured—no matter what your life circumstances are. I'm not saying that "everyone" will succeed as a leader, but we can certainly have far more leaders in our world than we currently do.

More leaders can be built if we just train and support them!

The good news is that it's never too late.

If you're someone who always slipped through the cracks growing up, I have a challenge for you. I want you to dare to be wrong. I want you to dare to make mistakes.

Today, I want to ask you to blindly step up for anything you can in your life. It doesn't matter if you don't know what you're doing, just step up.

- Start and lead a meetup in your area.
- Ask to be an assistant coach for a local children's sports team.
- Find a community program and volunteer to lead it.
- Go to your boss and ask to be involved in leading an activity unrelated to your daily job.
- Volunteer to lead a church group.

There are literally thousands of ideas.

The key is to just start. You don't have to have all the answers now - just do it.

I'm not saying this will be easy. Being a leader will require you to make some innate changes in yourself, and they will likely go against everything you were taught as a child.

There are five characteristics that I feel are the absolute most important to focus on when practicing your leadership skills.

Top Five Characteristics Of A Leader

Here are the top five characteristics of a leader that are the toughest to develop:

| ① CONFIDENCE & CONTROL | ② BECOMING SELFLESS | ③ DUPLICATING YOURSELF | ④ DELEGATING | ⑤ COMMUNICATION |

#1 - Confidence & Control

Leaders have to make decisions, period. Not only do leaders have to make decisions, they have to make these decisions fast. To top that off, leaders have to be ready to take responsibility and be accountable for their decisions!

Honestly, this can be the scariest thing about being a leader.

It all comes down to working on your *confidence*. A leader must have enough confidence in themselves to take control of a situation without having to think about it too much. When you can do this, everyone around you will quickly sense how you truly feel about what you're doing.

#2 - Becoming Selfless

The thing is that most of us have become very selfish over the years due to how our educational and professional systems are set up.

We're in an environment where our success depends on how others perceive us. Because of that, we like to take credit for the successes around us but quickly add distance when something goes wrong.

If something goes well - we did it. If something goes wrong, we had nothing to do with it.

The problem is that this is the exact opposite of what a great leader does.

True leaders are 100% selfless.

This means that a great leader steps up and gives full credit for a success to their team. However, when something goes wrong, a true leader steps up and takes full responsibility. They protect their team at all costs.

So, think about how important it is to you to be recognized for every good thing that you do. Letting go of that need will be one of the first things you need to do to master leadership as an Entrepreneur.

#3 - Duplicating Yourself

Here's another characteristic that many are deathly afraid of.

Throughout our childhood, we learn to strive to be the very best in what we do. Our competitive environment means that we have to make ourselves into a one-of-a-kind person with the end goal of being so valuable that a job or company literally can't run without us.
That translates into big paychecks, promotions, job security, etc...

However, again, this is the exact opposite of the way a leader thinks.

True leaders strive to make themselves completely irrelevant.

The goal of a great leader is to help their team grow. Their primary task is to build a machine that can run without them. The best way they can do this is to duplicate themselves as many times as possible. By that I mean they teach and support others to step up and take over certain jobs and tasks. They "duplicate" themselves, allowing them to hand off jobs one by one until they are no longer needed in the daily functioning of the team. Many times, leaders support their team members so much that the team members surpass the leader's own skills and talent.

It takes a truly selfless and confident leader to even have a chance of doing this without losing countless nights of sleep.

The more you look at truly successful Entrepreneurs, you'll find one very common trend. All successful Entrepreneurs surround themselves with smarter, more qualified people.

If they can't hire someone more qualified, they're helping someone grow to become more qualified than themselves.

#4 – Delegating

Delegation goes hand-in hand with duplicating yourself. Why? Because as you grow, one thing you'll learn fast is that you'll become your own biggest bottleneck. If you try to do it all yourself, your company is going to hit its ceiling very quickly.

This is why it's so important to duplicate yourself. The more talented people you have around you, the more critical tasks that you can delegate to others. The more tasks that you can delegate, the more your company can do!

With that said, even delegation has an art to it. It's not enough for a leader to just start assigning random tasks to team members. It goes way deeper than that. A great leader knows each and every one of their team members, and their strengths and weaknesses.

Proper delegation is knowing what to assign, to whom and when to assign it.

Not only are you better equipping your team members to succeed, but you're better equipping your company to conquer bigger mountains.

#5 – Communication

The fifth and final characteristic is communication.

Now, I'll be honest here. You need communication in every area of your life. Life is about the relationships we have with people, and communication is the foundation of each and every relationship.

I always say, "*He who can give bad news and make someone feel good about it is a leader who has mastered communication.*"

Anyone can deliver good news. The times that will count the most are the times when you have to deliver bad news.

Imagine sitting down with someone and telling them that they have not met their performance expectations. Or imagine sitting down and dealing with a conflict between two team members.

Now, imagine being able to face each of these circumstances head on in a way that leaves everyone feeling positive when they walk out of the room.

I know it sounds tough, but you have to start somewhere. The best Entrepreneurs in the world are able to lead thousands, if not millions, of people because of their ability to effectively communicate, inspire, and motivate.

Making A Conscious Decision

Since we aren't taught these five characteristics as we grow up, it's up to us to master them. The good news is that it's never too late to learn.

That means you have to make a conscious decision to develop these characteristics and skills in your life starting right now. This is why I say that leadership is learnable. It truly is.

Leadership is key for the sole reason that no dream worth having can be done alone. You'll need a team. And the minute you have a team, you'll need to sharpen your ability to lead them.

Dream Centers In India

I've had some pretty big dreams over the years, and perhaps the biggest one of all is a dream I've had since I was a child.

You see, I used to listen to my father tell stories about his childhood in India. He would talk about how he studied under street lamps or had to light candles because they had no electricity. Most of the children in his village didn't get very far at all (if they even started).

My father was forutnate that his father was relentless about helping his son prosper, but not all children have that kind of support.

For my father to be able to get an education, his entire family had to make immense sacrifices. Out of nine children, eight of them had to step back and focus on my father - that was the only way it would work. It always broke my heart to think that the rest of his brothers and sisters never got a great education.

On the positive side, look at what my father achieved by getting that education. He went on to move his family to the United States. He got a master's degree in nuclear engineering. He now works for the Nuclear Regulatory Commission (NRC) and is the government head of a nuclear power plant. Because of my father, I had such a privileged life - all thanks to him, his hard work, and his family's sacrifices.

Growing up, I kept thinking - *why did it have to be that way*? Why wasn't every child afforded the same opportunities as my father? What would happen if the millions of less fortunate children were just given a chance?

Hence my dream was born.

One day, I made a declaration. I even made it to my father. I said, "When I grow up, I'm going to build schools all over the world." Education should never be a privilege. It should be a birthright no matter where in the world you're born. I would make it my life's mission to make sure that every child had a fighting chance.

So, I decided that before I died, I would help *one million* children receive an education – children who would not otherwise have had the opportunity.

For a child with no money or know-how, that was one heck of a goal.

I didn't know how I would do it, but the goal was on my mind on a daily basis. The more I thought about it, the more I realized that I was going to need A LOT of help.

I held onto this dream for almost two decades. The day came when I started making a lot of money; when I could easily write a check and build 10 schools if I wanted to. But who would run them? Who would oversee them? Would my money be used in the way that I intended?

Money wasn't even 10% of the problem - again, I needed the right team, the right help and most importantly, the right partners.

Then in 2012, the most freakish series of events led me to the doorstep of an amazing couple in India. I went to their home to have tea for completely different reasons but discovered that fate had aligned us all along.

As it turned out, this couple, Naomi and Ian, had completely uprooted their entire family from the UK and moved to India with one dream: to build schools for children in the slums of Mumbai, India. Their biggest challenge was that they needed the funding.

And there began a beautiful team.

We rallied together as a team and within just months our first center (and school) was not only open, it was at 100% capacity. Shortly thereafter, we were building our second center, and then our third, and then our fourth. As of the day I'm writing this, we've built six centers and have three more in production. By the end of this year, we'll be supporting almost 1,000 children!

We like to call them Dream Centers because we're not just a school. We provide these children, and the entire community around them, with health clinics, dental clinics, tutoring, and Entrepreneurship training for women.

These are slum communities where many literally live in mud homes. Yet, thanks to this amazing team and their impeccable leadership, hundreds of lives are being transformed every year.

Remember, no dream worth having is one you can do alone - get yourself an amazing team.

Become A Leader Today

All you need to do is make a decision to be a leader and not a follower.

One decision to step up can not only change your life, it can have a profound effect on the world. But how do you do it? How do you become a leader?

It's like anything else – practice.

After all, how do you become a gardener? How do you learn to cook? You simply start doing it. You jump right in and practice until you get it. Leadership is no different.

Right now, I want you to make a declaration. I want you to say, "I am no longer going to shy away from opportunities. I'm going to raise my hand. I'm going to make mistakes. I'm going to have failures. I'm going to be embarrassed. I'm going to face my fears, but I choose to step up to lead. I choose to step up."

Go ahead, say it. *Choose* it.

It will be hard. You *will* make mistakes. But each time you do it, it will be a little less hard and you will make fewer mistakes. This process might take days or weeks. It might even take months or years.

But it's never too late. And you absolutely can do it!

Question Time

Once again, it's your turn to do some thinking about leadership in your life. Here are some questions for you to answer:

1. When you were in school and the teacher asked a question, were you the first to respond?
Did your hand shoot straight up or did you shy away from answering? I know I was always eager to answer questions in class. My hand would always fly up in the air.

2. Have you ever led a team?
This can be any team at all. A team or group in school, a team at work, a sports team, a volunteer team, or any other type of team.

3. Have you ever been in the middle of two people fighting and volunteered yourself to become the mediator? The one who puts it back together?
This can be a very awkward situation, especially if it's two friends or family members fighting with one another. Being impartial and not taking sides is the safe thing to do, but do you take it upon yourself to help them find a solution? Do you take charge and set a resolution in motion?

The answers to these three questions will give you a good idea of whether you choose to lead or choose to follow most of the time.

Remember, this is an incredibly important skill to develop as an Entrepreneur. Fortunately, if you're really uncomfortable with leadership, I will teach you a loophole you can use in Stage 4.

But for now, let's keep going with Stage 3 and explore the importance of **Taking Responsibility** in authority and leadership.

CHAPTER 23:
TAKING RESPONSIBILITY

"A good leader takes a little more than his share of the blame,
a little less than his share of credit."
– Arnold H. Glasow

Back in 2008, I had spent half a year preparing for a big product launch. That project was the first time I was ever fully reliant on my tech team, which was difficult for me because I'm not really a technical person. For that project, what it meant was that I had zero ability to guide them or check their work.

It was the biggest launch of my life, and I was 100% reliant on someone else's word. Not just me, but I had a ton of promoters and investors who were vested in my product launch.

As for me personally, I was responsible for the marketing and sales, and I felt at the time that I had done an amazing job. All systems were ready to go. Everything was set to go LIVE that Tuesday morning at 8:00 a.m.

I had more promotional support lined up than any other launch in my history, and things were looking promising.

Until the day played out...

7:50 a.m. – Perfect across the board, the countdown began...

7:53 a.m. – Looking strong and everything was going according to plan...

7:55 a.m. – My phone was blowing up with best wishes, and things were getting exciting...

7:57 a.m. – Wait, what was that – what just happened?

7:58 a.m. – "Guys, something weird is happening with the website. Someone check!"

7:59 a.m. – Full system crash. The entire website was 100% gone.

8:00 a.m. – Nothing. All systems down. All promotional traffic was going to a dead page.

I'll never forget that moment because it was the first time in my life that I literally lost six figures in the blink of an eye.

I personally did everything "right." I had prepared for months. I had implemented backups. Whatever I knew to do, I had done it. I had spared no expense.

I had genuinely given it my very best, but I was left with a very difficult decision to make.

Option #1 – Call the person leading my tech team and give him a piece of my mind. Shout, yell, blame, accuse. Then, let everyone in the world know who messed it all up to make sure my name was in the clear.

Option #2 – Start contacting all my top promoters and investors to get ahead of the crisis, rally the troops and figure out how to recover.

I know it's obvious which option was the right one, but it wasn't so easy to step up and do it in that moment. I truly wanted to just throw up and crawl under my desk.

But that's not what a leader does.

I knew that I had to take full responsibility and own every single thing that had happened. The only way I was going to fix the situation was by accepting responsibility for the problem. Excuses would do nothing but amplify the crisis.

So before anyone involved in the project even had a chance to call me, I was out ahead of it sending out mass texts, emails, phone calls – you name it. I was letting people know that I was in control and taking responsibility for fixing the problem.

I easily could have thrown my tech team under the bus and won some sympathy points...

...*But I didn't.*

Everything Comes Back To You

The truth is, it *was* my fault.

See, I *felt* that I did everything I could have, but that's obviously not true. There were an infinite combination of steps I could have taken that would have led to a very different outcome.

For starters, I should have seen early on that the person leading my tech team was inadequately prepared for the job. If I had seen that, I could have replaced him before things went south. I could have also asked more questions to those who actually built the application to find any inconsistencies in their answers.

What about the most obvious?

I could have insisted that we test the application first before launching.

There are an infinite number of things I could have done that would have stopped the system crash before it even started.

One of the hardest things about being an Entrepreneur is that *everything* comes back to you, and I mean *everything*.

- It's not the economy's fault.
- It's not the market's fault.
- It's not your competitor's fault.
- It's not your employee's fault.

The buck stops at the top, you. The reason why is simple. There is ALWAYS something you could've done differently to create a better result.

No Scapegoating Allowed

As humans we have been conditioned to blame others for our problems since biblical times. There's literally thousands of years of coding in our DNA for it.

The term many are used to hearing when we assign blame to others is *scapegoating.* It just so happens that this term first appeared in the Bible.

In ancient Judaism, each year on a major festival called Yom Kippur, two goats were chosen. One goat was slaughtered and given as a blood sacrifice to God. The other goat was known as the *scapegoat.* The sins of the people were symbolically laid on this goat and it was released into the wilderness, carrying the people's sins away with it.

Hence, even though humans committed the sins and wrongdoings, all blame and consequences were placed on this goat. This act freed people of all responsibility of their actions.

We have been trained to find ways to avoid taking responsibility for our actions for quite some time. Although this explanation may make us feel better about why we do what we do, we can't let it excuse how we continue to live.

Because I can promise you this…

You will NEVER get to the top as a leader if you are constantly blaming everyone else for what's happening around you. You absolutely must learn to be responsible, especially when things go wrong. That's when it counts the most.

In 1990, my family moved us from India to the United States. We came right back to where I was born – Maryland. The year we returned, everyone in our state was talking about only one thing: Our football team, the Washington Redskins.

I would watch my dad cheer weekend after weekend. I would see all my friends wearing Redskins jerseys. So, it was only natural that I became a big fan within weeks.

However, unlike all the other children who would roam around in jerseys of their favorite players, I seemed to be a big fan of a very unlikely candidate...

Joe Gibbs, the head coach of the Redskins.

Like the little football nerd I was, I loved watching the postgame press conferences and game recaps – all because the coach would come out and give his thoughts.

One evening, the Redskins had a huge victory. It was one of the best games I had ever seen. Everyone was on a high, the atmosphere was electric and I was waiting to see what the coach would say. He came out for the press conference and the media pounced on him.

Everyone was shaking his hand and congratulating him on a great win.

But what does Joe Gibbs do?

He stepped up to the podium and said, "Why are you congratulating me? I had nothing to do with this. This is all because of our amazing players, our amazing defense, our star offensive line and the MVP of the game, our quarterback. All these guys worked so hard and made this game amazing. We won because of them."

He took absolutely NO credit. He just complimented the team and walked away.

Unfortunately, the high from the win didn't last long.

The following week, the situation was reversed. The team had suffered an embarrassing loss to our biggest rivals. Everyone was upset. Instead of high fives and handshakes, everyone was wondering who was responsible for the loss.

As Joe Gibbs walked out, I expected him to do a big analysis of where the team went wrong and where they could improve, but he didn't. He walked out, took full responsibility, apologized and said, "I apologize to our fans. There was obviously something missing in our preparation for this game and we will not let it happen again. Our coaching staff will fully dissect this and make sure we learn from it. Again, I take full responsibility."

I was completely mesmerized by this. I mean, if the players were responsible for the win, then isn't it only fair to say that they were responsible for the loss?

Nope.

A true leader will NEVER let the team take the blame. And that's what this coach did. He essentially said, "If we lose, it's my fault. If we win, it's because of them."

Owning It Is Easier

Believe it or not, the whole concept of owning everything that goes wrong actually comes from a selfish place.

It literally makes life and recovery from disaster easier!

When you own your failure instead of passing the buck, you cut through all the crap and all the red tape. When you own it, you can immediately get to work fixing it. You don't have to wait around for anyone else, and you don't have to work hard to get others to agree with you. You just take responsibility and immediately start working to fix it!

Let me show you what I mean by this.

Back in 2013, I was set to do a big webinar that would include 17,000 people from all over the world.

And right in the middle of the webinar, the server crashed. The webinar went dead.

Thousands of people got kicked off, thousands more could no longer join and many people were left with a frozen screen. Assuming my math is correct, I was easily set to do $2 million in sales that night.

Imagine that, $2 million in sales in just two hours – it was amazing!

Yet, when all was said and done, I barely pulled out $400,000. I ended up doing just 20% of my potential earnings, and I lost at least $1.6 million that evening.

Again, this technically wasn't my fault because I wasn't even in the server room. I was in the middle of hosting the webinar.

But you know what?

That night, after the webinar ended, I had to send an email to everyone who had registered for the webinar to explain what happened. When I did, I took full responsibility.

And things got better.

Because I didn't sit and blame others, I was able to own the issue and get a solution in place fast. While my exhausted team rightfully went to sleep, I sat up, made phone calls, and figured out how to recover a majority of that $1.4 million in revenue.

By 6:00 a.m., I had a solution in place. By 8:00 a.m., we were back to market.

In the end, not only did I recover the losses, but we ended up exceeding our goals. I credit 100% of this to the fact that I wasted no time blaming others – I simply leapt to taking responsibility and owning the problem.

Now that you have a good understanding of the need to take responsibility, it's time to do some thinking. So, here are some questions for you to answer...

1. Think about the last time something went wrong. How did you handle it?
You have to be honest here because this is a tough one to own up to. Was your first reaction to blame someone else or did you take responsibility and *then* offer an explanation? Remember, you can ALWAYS offer an explanation, but first you have to take responsibility.

2. When you do something great, are you fast to take credit for it or do you first search for anyone else you can give credit to?
This is important. Do you remove yourself from the limelight and give credit where credit is due?

3. Do you truly believe that the buck stops at the top?
Do you believe that, no matter what, the responsibility *always* comes back to the leader?

When you take full responsibility for everything that happens, things will move faster. Productivity will go up, and you will be able to hone your instincts so that you can make decisions quickly.

With that in mind, let's take a look at the next chapter, which is all about **developing instincts.**

CHAPTER 24:
DEVELOPING INSTINCTS

"I rely far more on gut instinct than
researching huge amounts of statistics."
– Richard Branson

Very early on in my Entrepreneurial career, I had an opportunity to meet Tony Robbins.

Back then, my business had started to finally show some results. I was generating between $10,000 to $15,000 a month in sales, but I was stalled - no more growth. So, I started attending events and trying to meet new people.

In one event that I attended, I got a chance to join a small group of people in a private room. Before I knew it, in walked Tony Robbins. He gave a small talk and then did a quick meet and greet - just enough time for a few questions and some pleasantries.

During his talk, he was asked a very cliché question. When I first heard the question, I rolled my eyes without knowing that the answer would change my life forever.

The question was, "What's the number one piece of advice you can give someone about becoming successful?"

Just like my reaction to the question, Tony had a small chuckle before he dropped the hammer...

"You know, so many people look for a trigger. They look for the secret button they can push to create success, but the truth is that that button doesn't exist. Success lies in one simple thing, and that is your ability to make decisions. And not just to make decisions, but to make them fast."

I can't tell you why, but I felt a shift inside of me the moment I heard that. Initially, I didn't understand what he had said. *What do decisions have to do with success?* It felt like the most random advice, yet it completely moved me at the same time.

Tony went on to say that people will burden themselves with indecisiveness to the point of complete paralysis. So, out of the fear of doing the wrong thing, most people end up doing nothing.

Let's dissect this *decision* thing further...

The Race Car Driver

Imagine a racecar driver buzzing down a track at over 200 miles per hour surrounded by other cars all doing the same speed. Now, just imagine having to make a decision while surrounded by all of those cars. You don't have much time.

In fact, you have a fraction of a millisecond, and in that miniscule window of time your decision could completely change the outcome of the race.

Forget the race, a wrong decision could become a life or death decision! Such big decisions are being made repeatedly, and the worst part is that the driver simply doesn't have the luxury to take the time to think about what to do.

What about fighter pilots?

They move at speeds quadruple that of racecar drivers, and their every move can be the difference between life and death for both them and those around them.

Again, huge decisions, but decisions that they are forced to make fast.

Now, I can hear you thinking, *"These are all extreme examples! We're not racecar drivers or fighter pilots."* That's exactly where the problem lies. Because we're not physically forced to make fast decisions, we've become complacent in making no decisions.

One of the secrets to seeing amazing success as an Entrepreneur is to keep yourself in that level of urgency for each and every decision that you make. After all, your decisions may not be for your own life or death, but they certainly are for the life or death of your business.

Analysis Paralysis

Have you ever heard of the phrase *analysis paralysis*?

It means that your indecisiveness is so extreme that you literally become paralyzed. You stress so much about making the *right* decision that you analyze every nook and cranny of a decision.

You analyze your situation so much, ask so many people questions and collect so much data that you second-guess yourself no matter which option you look at.

And no decision means...no action. No action means...a dead business.

Now, committing to making decisions is understandable. However, why did Tony go out of his way to say, "*Make fast decisions*"? What does speed have to do with it?

Two words.

1. Execution
2. Competition

True Entrepreneurs have the serious advantage of not having red tape and bureaucracy.

They just think, plan, and DO.

Three Guys In a Garage In Israel

Would you believe that three guys in a garage in Israel were able to beat Nokia to releasing software that's changed the world?

While Nokia threw $8.1 billion into it, these guys just had themselves and three computers. They didn't have a dime of funding.

In March of 2007, Nokia announced the $8.1 billion acquisition of a company called Navteq. Nokia's goal was to build a navigation system that could detect traffic and other road conditions to help optimize a user's driving experience.

They bought this company because it had the widest network of road sensors installed all over the world. Nokia wanted to dominate the navigation world and surpass both Google and Apple.

So, Nokia sat around a table for months analyzing, plotting, planning and eventually using a huge chunk of their cash to make this acquisition.

At the same time, there were three guys sitting around their computers busy just executing. Their goal was to build an app for all kinds of phones that would allow users all over the world to report road conditions in LIVE time - all by clicking some buttons.

Because they would have an army of people to provide data, they didn't need all of the road sensors that Nokia had spent so much time and money acquiring.

They knew they were up against one of the largest companies in the world. They also knew that Nokia had just thrown $8.1 billion into the same idea. They had the best engineers, programmers, and analysts. Many Entrepreneurs would analyze this situation to death and abandon the dream.

However, these three ignored all of that and just chased their vision.

So, what was the result?

They created an application called Waze that has gone on to accrue more than 65 million active monthly users in over 185 countries. They eventually sold their app to Google for $1.15 billion.

Make decisions. Take action and just do it.

Overanalyzing your risks won't lead to breakthroughs that will change the world.

What If You Make The Wrong Decision?

The probability making bad decisions won't change whether you take a month or a day to make the decision.

So, why not just make the bad decisions faster? Doing so will leave you with more than enough time to pivot and fix your mistake.

Remember earlier in this book when we talked about having a good relationship with failure?

Well, here is when it comes into play. When you make quick decisions, you'll very likely make a decision that leads to you failing at something. That word, failure, is really what holds us back. It's that very fear that creates our over-analysis problem.

But what if you could remove that fear? Or even better, what if you could learn to celebrate your failures? How much easier would it be to make decisions?

Let me ask you a blunt question...

How many decisions do you make that are truly life or death? How many decisions do you make that are truly irreversible?

I can almost guarantee that there aren't many.

Actually, I would be surprised if any decisions that we make on a normal basis are really that serious. We just create stories in our minds that make them very serious.

So, what's the worst thing that happens if you make a bad decision?

You simply learn from it, grow from it, and can rest east knowing that you'll never make that mistake again.

The bottom line is you're going to make bad decisions in your life one way or the other. You might as well make them faster so you have enough time to fix them. That way, you also get a chance to learn a lot more a lot faster.

Logically, it suddenly makes perfect sense!

Learning To Follow Your Gut

Developing the ability to make instinct-driven decisions requires you to listen to your gut.

But what exactly does that mean?

When you come to a situation that requires you to make a decision, you're going to have your first "go to" feeling. That will be your initial "hunch."

My personal experience would say that following this hunch often leads to far better results than over-analysis.

But let me be clear…

I'm not saying that you shouldn't do any analysis. All decisions have to be made with respect to information gathered, but there will be a point after you're done that you'll need to make a DECISION.

After the initial investigation period, this is when your gut comes in.

If you really listen to yourself, watch yourself, and dial into your mind, you're going to experience a *reflex decision* that comes to you.

Here's the process I've seen for decision making…

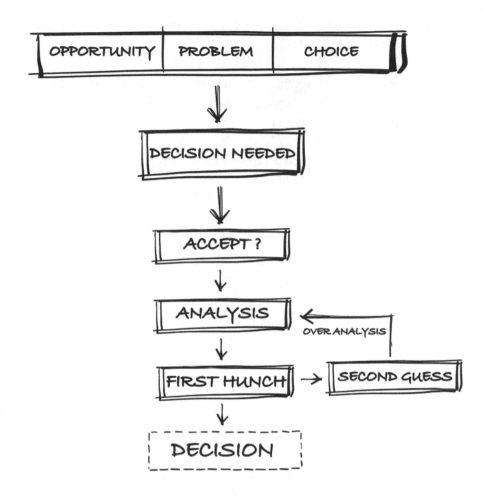

The key here is to stop at that first hunch. If you go beyond that, you're risking falling into the second-guess trap and starting the cycle of analysis paralysis.

Remember, even if your gut is off and you do the wrong thing, you can always pivot fast and fix it, but now you'll gain the gift of new knowledge!

The Billion Dollar Gut

One of my favorite "gut" stories is from one of the world's richest men, Warren Buffett. He's a prime example of someone who follows his gut instincts. He even does it when all the analysis in the market says the complete opposite of his gut!

Warren Buffett's first investment taught him to trust his gut no matter what was happening around him.

He made his very first investment when he was just 11 years old. He bought six shares of Cities Service (now CITGO) for $38 each. To this day, he doesn't know why. It just felt right.

Immediately after buying those shares, he watched the value plummet down to $27, wiping out 28% of his savings!

He thought about selling, which is what most people would have done. However, his instincts were saying otherwise. He decided to stay in it, even if it was against the conventional advice. Shortly after that decision, the stock climbed back up to $40.

Again, his gut told him to hold on. Unfortunately, he succumbed to "conventional wisdom" and sold the stock at $40, only to watch the stock climb to $202 just a few years later.

That was when Warren Buffett decided he would trust his gut and use patience. If his gut said one thing, he would be patient and let it have a chance.

Since that first stock, Warren now makes investment decisions based on his gut that are in the billions. He plays the long game. He trusts his instincts and hangs in there even when the market plummets or warns against his investments. He stays the course.

It goes without saying that his approach, although simple, has worked so well that he's now one of the richest men in the entire world.

Of course, this doesn't mean he makes rash decisions purely based on hunches. Remember the decision process. He still does his research and analysis. He knows when the right opportunity is, and he knows exactly what numbers to look for. However, he doesn't linger on a decision - once he has the data, he lets his instincts do the work.

Now, it's time for you to consider your own instincts by answering these questions:

1. What's the most recent decision you can remember debating for a long time?
Think about the last time you really took a long time to make a decision. Is this a normal way of decision-making for you, or is it rare?

2. When making a decision, do you naturally ask yourself, "So, what if this isn't right? What will I do?"
This is about whether you are cautious when you make your decisions or if you snap to it.

3. Do you tend to call a lot of people for council when making decisions?
Do you do this instead of being able to make a decision on your own?

We mentioned above that making fast decisions involves some risk, but that doesn't mean entrepreneurs are risk-takers. You'll see what I mean in the next chapter—**Calculated Risk-Taking.**

CHAPTER 25:
CALCULATED RISK-TAKING

"I talk a lot about taking risks, and then I follow that up very quickly by saying, take prudent risks."
– Irene Rosenfeld

Back in 2008, I decided to really go BIG. I had a brilliant idea. I was going to build a platform that disrupted the education world in the same way that Facebook disrupted social media.

Although it was a great idea, it almost killed me.

It was this very platform that led me to scaling my team, opening three offices around the world, and basically landing myself in $1.7 million in debt.

So, was it just a bad idea?

Actually, the idea itself was great (you'll see why in a bit). The problem was that it wasn't such a brilliant idea for ME because...

- I had no experience in the field that the idea was in.
- The idea had nothing to do with my business at that time.
- There was nothing like it on the internet to model or research.

All I had was, the idea.

But I still believe that the idea itself was full of opportunity, even if it wasn't for me.

I also discovered later that, as I was bleeding out hundreds of thousands of dollars trying to build my idea, there were a couple of guys sitting in their apartments in Turkey building a platform that was virtually identical to what I wanted to build.

While I was completely unprepared, unqualified, and in way over my head, these two guys were the perfect fit to create what ended up being called Udemy. Today, Udemy is valued at billions of dollars and is leading the private online education space.

All I Had Was an Idea

The problem was that when I did all of this and decided to make millions in investments...

- I had no clue how this platform would make money.
- I had no clue how I was going to fund it.
- I had no clue how I was going to build the technology.
- I wasn't even a technical person.
- I had no one on my team that knew how to do it.

I just started throwing money at an idea—there was no strategy or plan behind it. All I had was excitement for my idea. At that time in my life, there wasn't a single chance you could tell me that my idea was bad or risky.

I was 100% confident!

It was this exact thinking that led my life to unraveling.

I literally lost everything I had worked so hard to build because I had taken a huge UNCALCULATED risk.

Entrepreneurs Are NOT Risk-Takers

What I did is NOT what successful Entrepreneurs do.

You see, there is a myth out there that says Entrepreneurs are risk-takers. In fact, it's more than a myth. If you Google the word Entrepreneur, the word risk is actually in the definition.

> *"A person who organizes and operates a business or businesses, taking on greater than normal financial risks in order to do so."*

To make matters worse, we hear *glorified* stories all the time about some rogue Entrepreneur who went "all-in." We hear, "Oh, he put everything into it. It was a big gamble and then he became a multi-billionaire."

But people just say that.

Never do they stop to wonder, "*Wait. Did he really just blindly go in? Maybe it wasn't a big gamble. Maybe that guy actually made a smart decision and knew what he was doing.*"

Without questioning what we hear, the misconception keeps building up in all of our minds. Well, the same thing was happening with me. I actually thought that blindly going all-in was making me into an admirable Entrepreneur.

"*Boy, my story is going to be amazing...*"

Well, lesson learned.

The more Entrepreneurs I meet, the more I understand the fundamental difference between what society thinks Entrepreneurs do and what they actually do.

Entrepreneurs are NOT uncalculated risk-takers. Entrepreneurs are certainly not gamblers, not even close.

Entrepreneurs that reach the top and stay there aren't putting everything on the line, crossing their fingers and hoping for the best. Yes, many people see Entrepreneurs putting everything into one company or one idea, but they don't see all the research and preparation that went into their decision.

In the end, what they're doing is taking a *calculated* risk.

Right Idea, Wrong Timing

The success of Udemy has proven that the idea I had all those years ago for an open education platform was worth billions of dollars. Udemy now has 65,000 courses and has raised multiple rounds of venture capital.

The same idea was equally good and equally stupid for two different people. For me, it was a stupid way to go.

Given how little I knew about technology, coding and development, the entire idea was risky from the first day. I had to invest a lot of money and blindly trust someone else to get my platform built.

However, the founders of Udemy could sit around a laptop, bang out code and control the entire process themselves.

For me, because of all the money I was investing into the development, monetization was super important and had to be done super early in the process. I continued to build blindly even though I had no idea how to monetize.

However, the founders of Udemy were putting in sweat equity instead of loads of money. As long as they could afford to live, they weren't hard pressed to create monetization!

So, yes, the idea was great, but what you need to take into account is TIMING. For me, at that time, it was a horrible idea.

Although I failed miserably at building Lurn the first time around, times are different today. I have access to more resources. I'm wiser. I'm smarter. I know what I'm doing this time.

So, as of two years ago - we declared we're building the Lurn platform again.

However, this time it's going to be very different than I had originally planned. This time, I've done it all right. We have a brilliant tech team. I know just how to monetize. I have all the contacts I need. Everything is in place the way it should be.

This time, we're not competing with Udemy at all. Instead, we're evolving and going after a very specific target niche that is our core competence.

I got strategic. I got tactical. I got calculated.

Along with rebuilding the online Lurn platform, I decided to also start building another dream of mine, the Lurn Center.

When they first heard about this idea, many people around me thought I must've gone crazy. They wondered why I would risk making the same mistake I made before. Why would I ever "*blindly*" invest over $3 million putting up an entire building?

To be honest, my investment is A LOT more than just $3 million. That's just what it cost to get the center opened. I've signed a 10-year lease and still have to pay for:

- Rent
- Utilities
- Employees

All in, I'm probably looking at a total cost of $1 million a year just to run the facility. So, really, that's over $10 million you can add to the $3 million.

Sound crazy yet?

Yes, there is some risk here, but the key thing is that it's CALCULATED risk and here's why...

#1. Half of the initial $3 million is not being paid by me. Instead, the landlords are covering it because they are giving me that much money to build the place out the way I want.

So that leaves me with $1.5 million that I have to cover myself.

#2. Because $1 million of that $1.5 million is equipment, we got a bank to finance it. I have no personal guarantee involved and it was pretty straightforward (the loan is secured by the equipment behind it).

So, now that leaves me with $500,000 to pay.

#3. The remaining $500,000 is what I saved up myself over the last three years. I put money away every month so that I could cover this cost.

Thus, I minimized my entry risk to just $500,000.

In addition, I worked out a deal where I have a certain amount of time when I don't have to pay rent. It just so happens that the amount of free rent I got ends up equaling almost exactly $500,000!

Go figure.

But my calculated thinking is not done yet. Let's continue and talk about that $1 million a year I have to invest in running the facility.

#4. I was spending about $12,000 a month in a ridiculously overpriced co-working space. Now that's gone. That's about $144,000 that I was already spending.

This brings us down to $856,000 that I have to figure out.

#5. We were doing about five events per year in hotels. Each event would cost us about $150,000 to host at the hotel. Guess what? We no longer have to pay hotels because we can host these events in our facility. So, that totals to $750,000 in costs I was already spending.

This brings us down to $106,000 that is left to figure out.

#6. In the first year that the facility is launching, we are planning to host about 25 events in the new building (and that number is growing fast). Last year, we only did five events. This year, we can do almost as many as we want!

Tell me something…

Doesn't it seem like a wise investment to put $106,000 into a facility that allows me to do as many LIVE events as I want? When you do the math, I would have been stupid to NOT invest in this facility.

On their own, ideas are worth nothing. They're just ideas. But…

Calculated Risk + Great Idea = Success

Let's face it. EVERYONE has ideas.

There is no shortage of people dilly dallying and dreaming of building the next big thing. But most people are just too scared of the risk to actually try fighting for their dream.

Heck, they're even too scared to sit down and do the risk-calculation. It's too uncomfortable for them. They'd rather just make Excel files, talk big, get excited and wait until the adrenaline dies down and move onto the next idea.

I call these guys Excel Entrepreneurs.

What they don't realize is that money doesn't come from ideas; it comes from smart execution.

Sendlane

I have a good friend, Jimmy Kim, who recently made a very gutsy decision that changed his life – he sold all his businesses and put all his eggs in one company, Sendlane. The craziest part is that he made the decision right around the time he was having his first child.

So, is he just a raging cowboy with nerves of steel?

Not at all. No matter what was happening in his life at the moment, it never impacted his approach to making the decision - no matter how crazy it was.

Here's what Jimmy did.

He saw so much potential in how Sendlane was growing that he decided to double down and commit all his time to that one company alone. He even sold his other companies at a deep discount, losing money on some – he just wanted to move fast and transition. His analysis was strong, and he just wanted to get on with his new life.

I'll admit that initially when he told me, even I wasn't completely convinced. I called him crazy at least once or twice.

But Jimmy plowed on, sold all his cash-generating businesses, rolled up his sleeves, dove in and became the CEO of just one company. He literally did the opposite of what every financial guru recommends and put ALL of his eggs in just one basket.

But, just BEFORE he made the decision to sell everything, he showed me his calculations. He showed me his analysis and research. I realized then that he wasn't crazy at all, he truly had strong evidence that showed that this "*gamble*" was in his favor.

So, what happened?

Just months later Sendlane.com has DOUBLED in revenue. He's having to get more office space. He's happier. He's making more money. And, most of all, he's living his dream.

While most will go around thinking he took a crazy risk and went "all in," those around him know that he was actually very smart and calculated about it!

Focus On The Word "Calculated"

When talking about risk, remember that the main word to focus on is **CALCULATED**. That is the *only* type of risk that is acceptable.

You need to sit down and go through all the ins and outs of what you want to do. I'm not a big fan of business plans, but I am a big fan of knowing the answers to the most important questions, such as:

- Can you handle it if something goes wrong?
- How are you going to develop this?
- How will you market this?
- Who are the people you need to make it work?
- Do you have access to these people?
- Can you afford these people?
- If you lost every penny that you put into this, what would it do to your life and to your family?

If any of these answers are extreme, then it's not the right idea or time for this risk. And that's OK! Don't get so attached to your idea that you create fake data and scenarios to start justifying your decisions.

There are a million ideas out there. The key is to find a good idea that is both the right fit for you and the right time.

Question Time

Now it's time for you to do a self-assessment by answering these questions:

1. Have you ever thought through an idea and decided not to do it because of everything that you had on your plate at the time?
Have you ever actually sat down and said, "You know what, I'm doing too much already. I'm not going to do this."

2. When you have an idea, do you sit down and actually plan it out?
Do you have an idea and actively take time—days or months—to plan it out and ask questions?

3. Do you know how to create a marketing plan?
I honestly feel that when it comes to calculated risk-taking, the number one thing that most people miss is creating a marketing plan.

One thing that is no longer true - to any degree - is the saying, "*Build it and they will come.*" This one saying alone could fill a graveyard of amazing businesses that never made it because the Entrepreneur behind them never thought about how they would actually get their customers.

If there's one thing you spend the most time on, make it your marketing plan.

With this lesson, we come to the end of Stage 3, Authority. By now, you should have a solid idea of what you need to work on in this authority stage to help you become the leader you need to be—to have authority over yourself and others.

It's now time to move on to the final and critical stage for any Entrepreneur —Stage 4, People.

STAGE 4: PEOPLE (P)

CHAPTER 26:
P – PEOPLE

"It's really important to have those people
in your life who push you to be better, different."
– Jesse Peyronel

When I started out as an Entrepreneur in 2003, there were actually two versions of me.

The physical me and the virtual me.

Both versions felt the same and thought the same - we were the same in every way. Yet, the people around me and the environments of the two versions were incredibly different.

The physical me was surrounded by people who were very different from me. I simply didn't have Entrepreneurs around me. I didn't have people me who thought a little crazy like me. I didn't have any dreamers or fantasizers around me.

The physical me was surrounded by doctors, engineers, and lawyers.

All of the guidance, leadership and mentorship I was receiving at the time was not resonating with me - there was a great disconnect, and I could feel it daily.

I felt that any time I talked about what I *truly* wanted - my dreams, my business, Entrepreneurship - I was discouraged. The people around me would warn me of all the bad things that could happen. They would tell me that I wasn't ready. They would tell me to "stay on track" and let the system work.

I heard it. It even made sense most days. However, every night before I went to bed, something just wouldn't connect with me. Something felt wrong.

Then there was virtual me.

This is the me that decided to turn to Google and type in "how to make money online." Virtual me found myself in the exact opposite environment of physical me.

I ended up in an online forum full of people who were just like me! The only difference between us was that they weren't just dreaming - they were actually out there making things happen.

I was very fortunate that I found this community early on in my career. Even though I have never met (face to face) any of my early supporters on this forum, their influence on the *virtual me* turned me into who I am today. Thanks to what I heard and saw them doing, I was able to see that there was another option.

They proved to me that I could indeed dream big. They showed me that I wasn't crazy.

And that was the spark that led me to finally following my passion.

Connection Fuels Success

Most struggling Entrepreneurs never end up finding this connection. They never find a community they can plug into for support. Unfortunately, most Entrepreneurs are forced to go at it alone. The problem is that they end up living in an environment surrounded by fear, negativity, and warnings.

It's amazing how impactful our surroundings can be, even if they are virtual.

At our core, humans are a *social species* - we need comradery, community, feedback, and support. So, it goes without saying that we embrace and become whatever we surround ourselves with.

I think back to my own success.

Had I not turned to Google one day and found my way to this online forum, there is almost zero chance that I would have ever made it. I would have probably become a miserable, mediocre doctor practicing for the sole purpose of "making good money."

In this stage, we're going to take a deep dive into your environment. You'll get a chance to really dissect whether your surroundings are giving you a fighting chance at succeeding as an Entrepreneur.

Not Bad, Just Different

Now, I need to point out that physical me didn't have a *bad* environment—it was simply DIFFERENT.

The people in my life weren't bad people. They weren't trying to hurt me. Actually, most of them were very dear friends who loved me and were just trying to protect me from getting hurt. They were speaking to me out of love. They were speaking to me with the knowledge and wisdom that they themselves had access to.

The problem was that they just weren't empowered with the knowledge or background to be able to support me. They were the wrong people for me to seek advice from.

I now realize that asking them for advice on how to become an Entrepreneur was as ridiculous as asking an architect how to perform brain surgery. However, this is what most of us do. We turn to the people closest to us to help guide us, even if they aren't the most qualified.

But, again, always remember that just because the environment around you may not be giving you the best advice, it doesn't mean that it's a bad or negative environment.

You'll need to learn how to recognize this fast so you can take control of your surroundings.

Jim Rohn once said, "*You are the average of the five people you spend the most time with.*"

He wasn't wrong. The Association of Psychological Science did a study that found that people who had friends who had more self-control tended to have more self-control themselves.

Other research published in The New England Journal of Medicine shows that people who are friends with obese people are 57% more likely to become obese themselves. This is a behavioral trait that can literally be passed from one person to the next.

Why?

Because fitting in is a human need.

Abraham Maslow came up with his hierarchy of needs in 1943. In this hierarchy, there are a total of five needs that are still recognized today. These are the basic needs that every human has.

First...
Physiological - the need for things like food, water, and air.

Second...
Safety - the need to feel safe and secure.

Third...
Love and belonging - the need to feel accepted by the people around you.

Notice this third need. Yes, this is an actual NEED. You need connection and companionship. It's the third most important requirement, just above food and water and safety.

The only conclusion is that it may be a good idea to surround yourself with a group of successful Entrepreneurs if you want to become an Entrepreneur.

The main aim of this stage is not to start removing people from your life (like many of the gurus teach). Instead, I'm going to show you how to build a supportive environment around yourself.

Just as importantly, this doesn't mean that you'll now start trying to convince the people who don't understand you to suddenly change and start supporting you. This is wasted energy, and it won't work 99% of the time.

Instead of trying to change everyone around you, you're going to go out and start finding the right people to balance the influence in your life (just like I did with the virtual me).

There are two major steps you'll take to re-craft your environment:

#1 - Evaluate the people currently in your life. Create specific communication plans with each one of them. Doing this means that you are taking full control of just how much influence each person in your life will be allowed to have on you.

#2 - Start adding the right kinds of people into your life.

The Internet Has Become My Greatest Tool!

Recently, a student at our Lurn Masters event, Danny, asked me a great question when I was on stage. He asked, "I don't have any Entrepreneurs in my local area that I can connect with for support. How did you do it? How did you find people locally to support you?"

Now, this was incredible. It was the first time I had ever been asked this question and I stood there frozen. I was stunned because, as I thought about my answer, I couldn't believe what I was about to say…

Here I was, a successful Entrepreneur with 15 years of experience and near $200 million in sales, and guess what?

I still didn't have any local support around me.

If you had put a gun to my head and asked me to call a local Entrepreneur who I masterminded with or even went for drinks with, I wouldn't have a single person.

Don't get me wrong. I have very supportive people in my life. I have an amazing wife, brilliant parents, an awesome family and superb friends - they love me and support me.

But not a *single* one of them is an Entrepreneur.

I couldn't believe it. I was still living with the *physical me* and the *virtual me*, yet it didn't matter - I was still experiencing great success!

I realized it doesn't matter if you have local Entrepreneurial support. As long as you have the internet, you can still build the environment you need!

We live in a global marketplace today. Everyone is connected to everyone, so you're just a few clicks away from the people that you need in your life - no excuses!

In fact, this is the exact reason why we've built such a strong #LurnNation community.

It's Your Responsibility

In the end, the people in your life are your responsibility. Your surroundings are your responsibility. It's up to you to build your surroundings the way *you* want them.

And the five elements we will cover in Stage 4 will help you do that. These elements are:

217

1. Analyzing The People In Your Life
2. Grow Your Network
3. Negative People And What To Do With Them
4. Ask Questions, Seek Answers
5. Mentorship

As we go through these five elements, you'll learn how to build an environment around you that will help you thrive. So, let's start by first doing one of the hardest things you can - analyzing the people who are currently in your life.

CHAPTER 27:
ANALYZING THE PEOPLE IN YOUR LIFE

"Today...spend more time with people
who bring out the best in you, not the stress in you."
– Unknown Author

"Are you sure that's a good idea?"

"Absolutely," I said.

"It sounds risky. I don't think you should do it."

"I've checked it all out. I know it's a good idea. I know it'll work."

"I really think you shouldn't do it. I don't like all this risk."

"I'm telling you it's safe. I've done my research."

"So? Is it really necessary that you take all this risk at all?"

This conversation went on for 20 minutes - we were at a deadlock. After a few minutes, it even started to get me a bit down. I had been so excited but now I was having second thoughts. Heck, I almost didn't do the project at all because of this conversation.

In any other light, you would think the person I was talking to was being negative, right? Well, this person I'm talking about is now my wife!

She's the single best thing that has ever happened to me. She has supported me in ways that I never imagined possible, and there is zero chance I would be where I am today without her by my side.

Had I listened to the "gurus," that one conversation alone could have led me to think maybe this won't work out. I assure you that if it hadn't worked out, I wouldn't be writing to you today.

My wife was not being negative. She was being a loving, cautious, and protective partner. She was truly concerned about me. The protective side of her was trying to nurture me away from doing anything that had even 5% of risk. That's all. She just didn't understand what I was trying to do.

We hear so often that we should eject the negative people from our lives, but many people take this too far. This doesn't mean that you should let go of every person who doesn't agree with what you're doing.

This conversation with my wife took place early in our relationship. She didn't come from an Entrepreneurial background, so she was thinking with a very different hat on than I was. Instead, her background taught her that job *security* was very important and that risk was to be avoided at all costs.

Now, given time to get to know me, my surroundings and the way my mind works, suddenly she's not only supporting my crazy ideas, she's got her hands, feet, and legs right in there with me!

I can't even stand the thought of imagining what my life would have been like without her. So, let's set the record straight...

Learn To Recognize The Negative People

Back then, my wife was simply trying to protect me. That's all. She wasn't being negative. She was just worried about me.

You cannot cut out all the people from your life who are worried about you and are just trying to protect you. Just think about who you would have left if you did that. It could literally destroy your life if you did a blanket removal of the people in your life you thought were negative.

Why?

Because these are the people who care the most about you.

Instead, you need to learn to analyze the people in your life so you can determine who really is negative and who is just being protective.

Since I don't believe in ejecting someone from your life just because they seem negative, I came up with what I call the **Circle of Support:**

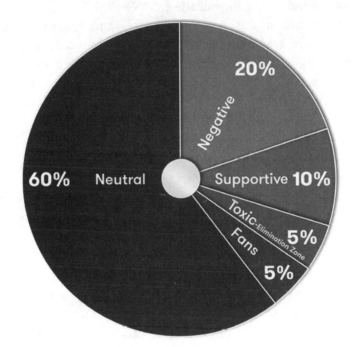

Now, I didn't do an elaborate scientific study to create this diagram. Instead, I relied on decades of brutal life experience.

Also, having coached thousands of people from all over the world, I can say with a lot of confidence that this Circle of Support stands the test of time.

- **5% of the people in your life can be considered "True Fans."**
  They are truly committed to you no matter what you do. They look at you and see a world of possibilities. They'll always support you even if they think you're a little crazy. Keep these people very close to you and make them the first people that you lean on for support or encouragement.
- **10% of the people in your life are "Supportive."**
  They are the people who are closest to you. They might not believe in everything you want to do, and they may even think

you're crazy, but they'll support you and try to help you however they can. This is a good group of people to bounce ideas off of when you want to hear the other side of things. This group can really help you get "balance" in your thoughts.

- **60% of the people in your life are "Neutral."**
This is most of the people in our lives, and this isn't a bad thing. They aren't as close to us as the supportive people, and they probably spend more time thinking about their own goals and dreams than they do thinking about yours. They are not bothered by what you're doing or not doing because it doesn't impact them. Hence, they don't really support or stop you - they're just there.

Honestly, these are the people that you hang out with when you need to get away from your dreams and goals. Whether you just need a night out or something fun to do, your neutral friends play a pivotal role in helping to keep you sane!

- **20% of the people in your life are likely "Negative."**
These people are usually pretty close to you. You see them often, spend decent time with them and you trust them for the most part. However, they can be vocally negative towards your "crazy" goals and dreams. They offer you caution, warnings and tell you all the things that could go wrong.

These are the people with whom you need to really sharpen your people skills. Rather than just removing them from your life, you have the opportunity to learn how to better communicate with them. You can selectively choose what you share and what you don't share with them. Most of the time, "negative" people are just being that way to protect you. However, if their intentions pivot to wanting to hurt you, they become toxic.

- **5% (MAX) of the people in your life are going to be what I call "Toxic."**
These are the people who are flat out trying to hurt you. These can be very damaging people in your life. They soak up your energy and may even be rooting for you to fail for several reasons. When it comes to removing people from your life, it's these toxic people that have to go. No argument or discussion to be had.

Everyone OTHER than the toxic people not only *can* stay in your life, but likely *should* stay in your life. All of these people serve their own purpose, and they never mean ill for you deep down. The key to making sure that they never impact you negatively is up to you - you just need to learn how to manage them better instead of removing them.

Who's Negative & Who's Toxic?

I learned way back in those early days that, when I have a "crazy" idea, I have to be selective of who I share it with and what exactly I share with them. Just because you're declaring your dreams doesn't mean that every person in your life needs access to every detail.

So, negative people are up to you to manage.

We do it through being selective of who we share what with. By simply being more selective in your conversations, you can quite easily take a negative person and turn them into a supportive person. Take a moment to really learn more about them, their upbringing, their background, and their own patterns of thinking.

This way, every piece of advice or "negativity" they give you, you'll have a great filter to put it through. You'll start to learn what parts of your life that specific person is empowered to support you and what parts they just aren't.

Again, it will come down to your control and your choices.

But before we do any of that, let's start by figuring out whether a person in your life even deserves that time.

One of the most toxic people I ever had in my life...

Years ago, I met a person in India who quickly became a great friend of mine. This was one of the smartest people I had ever met. His brain was amazingly wired to seek out solutions to almost any problem. Before I knew it, he was helping me conquer some of the biggest challenges of building a big team in India.

One thing led to another and we decided to start working together in an official capacity. We came up with a good deal for both of us, and we decided that he would be the President of Operations in India. Very quickly, I gave him a big role in my company.

I started to trust him with my finances. I started to give him full authority. I started to give him bigger and bigger projects. I really did let him run the India operations as if it were his own company. Even when I didn't agree with some of his decisions, I had so much faith in him that I let him do whatever he wanted.

Well, over the course of years, some things started to not add up.

As I was going through a horrible financial situation, I started to uncover some very problematic things in the company. Fast forward and I came to learn that this man was flat out robbing me. He had been doing it for years.

He was the textbook definition of a conman. He had been methodically laying his traps for me from the very first day we met and, as trusting as I was, I fell for it all.

I went on to discover that he had...

- Methodically lied to me about other people in my life so that I would come to rely on him.
- Hired bad employees on purpose to take more money from me.
- Been skimming off the top of almost every financial transaction our company did - from rent to internet to the employees I was hiring.
- Stolen money from our transactional accounts to the tune of tens of thousands a month.

Once I did my research, I actually found over 23 ways that he had been stealing from the company.

I remember just how nasty it all got when I discovered this. Not only was I heartbroken, but I was embarrassed and angry at myself. I couldn't believe that I had let someone take advantage of me at such a level.

This person deserved the worst that I could bring to him. He was downright evil and my life would be better off if I never saw his face again.

I got the police involved. I got lawyers involved. I was just hours away from getting the Indian media involved as well before he and I finally came to a settlement.

The bottom line here is that he's an example of a person who was truly toxic and deserved to be completely removed from my life.

In my opinion, people need to be actively trying to hurt you if you're going to remove them from your life completely. They need to be someone that provides zero (or even negative) value to your life.

In the end, differentiating between a toxic and negative person comes down to two things:

#1 - Their intention. Are they being "negative" to hurt you or because they're worried about you?

#2 - The value they provide in your life. Let's say I'm walking down the street and a passerby is being negative. There's no benefit to trying to keep that person in my life, so I can just walk away.

The more you learn about "people management," the more you'll realize that it really is all about how *you* react to the situation.

Negative people can be managed.

First, learn to decipher who gets to stay in your life. Second, figure out just how much they need to know about your goals and dreams.

Quality, Not Quantity

You have to remember that the number of people in your life isn't what is important.

It's the QUALITY of these people that's important.

By nature, most Entrepreneurs will keep their circle of friends very small. There are two reasons for this. One is that they just don't have the time for a lot of people in their life. They don't have the time for parties, bars, happy hours, and socializing. The second reason is that smart Entrepreneurs work hard to actively protect their environment.

Personally, I have a very small group of friends. These friends would step in front of a train for me, and I would do the same for them. These are also friends who I can easily talk to about my crazy ideas and goals. I can trust that they'll never underestimate my abilities and that they'll actually push me to achieve more.

They'll extend their own networks to me. They'll dive in and help me. They'll mastermind with me, and they'll even protect me if I mess up.

Trust me, being an Entrepreneur and building a circle such as mine is the equivalent of having a super power. This kind of support opens you up to a lot more opportunity and risk-taking than you could have ever imagined.

So, when building your environment, think about the *quality* of your circle instead of how big it is.

Question Time

Once again, it's time to answer a few questions to start evaluating what kind of environment you've built around yourself. Answer the following questions honestly:

#1 - Do you have any toxic people in your life?
This is the most urgent consideration. Are there people in your life right now that you can confidently say are truly trying to hurt you? If the answer is yes, these people have to go - period.

#2 - Does the person closest to you support you?
This can be your spouse, parents, or best friend. The person in your life who is closest to you—do you have their support? If not, you need to consider why that is. It may even be time to sit down with them and have

a heart to heart. Maybe you're oversharing with them. Maybe they're not understanding you correctly. Maybe they're not even aware that you consider them to be unsupportive. Talk to them and find out what's going on.

#3 - How large is your social circle?
I really want you to take a moment to evaluate the answer to this question. Do you have a lot of close friends or just a few? Consider how this impacts your life, your time, and your ability to focus on your dreams and goals.

This can be the hardest question to deal with at times, but I'll leave it with you now that you know what you need to do!

Alright, so we talked about how it's important to keep a small social circle. Now let me give you the opposite advice about your network.

Let's move on to the next chapter to understand the difference between a social circle and your professional network. Let's dive into why **Growing Your Network** is so important.

CHAPTER 28:
GROWING YOUR NETWORK

"The richest people in the world look for and build networks,
everyone else looks for work. Marinate on that for a minute."
– Robert Kiyosaki

One time when I was onstage giving a talk, someone asked me, "How do you have such an amazing team, and how do you know so many important people?"

This question caused a serious moment of reflection for me—I took a moment to think about ALL the people I've had the honor of meeting throughout my life.

I realized just how blessed I've been because of the people around me.

The list of freakish coincidences in my life is actually pretty amazing:

1. The most influential book I have ever read is *Rich Dad, Poor Dad*. This book literally changed who I am at the core. The author of this book is Robert Kiyosaki, and I grew up idolizing him. I hoped that one day I could meet him just to shake his hand and thank him.

    Now, I've not only met him, but I'm actually business partners with him. He even calls me to ask for advice! It still leaves me speechless whenever my phone rings and I see his name.

2. Growing up, I read a lot about Sir Richard Branson and was always flabbergasted by his success. It was enough for me just to be able to meet him and shake his hand, but now I've actually been to his home and sung with him on a table like a couple of madmen. The man is absolutely full of life.

3. My entire life, I was surrounded by Bollywood movies featuring an actor by the name of Shah Rukh Khan, he was considered a legend in the industry. Well, I've now met him, done business with him, been to his home, and had dinner with him.

I'm telling you, the list goes on. The person who asked me that question was right. How in the world have I been able to do this? The most important thing to know is that it's neither luck nor coincidence that I've met these people.

Although there's no step by step "system" that led me to connecting with Robert Kiyosaki or Sir Richard Branson, there is absolutely a foundational function that I can credit this success back to.

Growing My Network

The underlying foundation of every relationship I've developed and every team member I've brought onboard is this…

Growing my network.

I've grown my network by meeting people in person, over the phone, through email, through Facebook messages, and even through social media tags. In fact, a lot of my amazing Lurn team members are here solely because I connected with them on Facebook or LinkedIn.

So what does it mean to grow your network?

It's simple.

It just means growing the number of people you know and the number of people who know you. The simplest way I track this is by watching my phone. I believe that if I have someone's cell phone number, then I know them enough and they recognize who I am.

As long as the number of contacts in my cell phone is growing, I can rest easy knowing that my network is growing.

So, how exactly do I meet people?

There are several ways:

- Introductions from my existing network...
- Events and conferences...
- Educational events...
- Customers and students who visit us...
- Carpenters, electricians and plumbers who do work for us...
- Doormen at local 5-star hotels...
- Taxi drivers in India when I visit...

In short, I meet people everywhere.

The list of how you can grow your network is endless, especially today with the internet and social media. Even if you're shy or quiet, you can easily make new contacts, anywhere, anytime.

Just remember that every single person you meet can impact your life, your goals, and your dreams in amazing ways. But you'll never know how much until you start talking to them.

Your Network Is Your Net Worth

There is a *direct* relationship between your network and your net worth.

Even if you are just acquainted with people or follow them on Facebook, they're still part of your network.

I recently did an evaluation of the people in my network. I looked at the contacts in my cell phone. I looked at my LinkedIn and Facebook profiles. I looked everywhere and made an estimation of how many people I know and how my network has grown over the years.

I also tracked my revenue over that same time period.

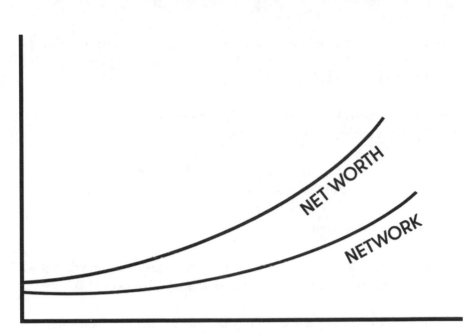

You can see in the graph that there is a correlation between the number of people I know and the revenue of my companies.

The general shape and trend of this graph proves a direct relationship between network and net worth.

The other thing I want you to notice is how your network can grow exponentially. The first 100 people you meet in your life will always be the hardest. However, it gets easier and easier after that. The reason is that the people in your network have their own network.

Before you know it, you won't even have to know someone directly to get help with a problem or a question that you have. You'll be able to reach out to your network to come up with a contact that can solve your problem. It's pretty amazing how quickly this happens.

Take this example. I was looking for an audiovisual company that could run our events. We wanted a very specific type of company, and we had already burned about $100,000 trying to find the right one. After failing to find the right fit, I decided to post on my Facebook wall.

"I'm looking for a great A/V company to run our events.
Please tag someone if you know anyone."

I connected with five of the best companies in our industry within 24 hours. Within 72 hours, I made a deal with an amazing company that continues to do incredible work for us to this day.

Just think - all that started with a quick post on my Facebook wall. It took me maybe 30 seconds to write that post.

The bottom line is that the more people you know, the easier your life is, the faster you solve problems, and the more money you end up making.

Never Make Assumptions

One of the greatest mistakes we make when we meet someone is that we often immediately judge them and their potential value in our life.

If I hadn't learned my lesson on what makes that so problematic, I wouldn't have met half of the wonderful people in my life.

For example...

- I was once approached by a person making wild claims of his access. I didn't believe him initially because it sounded so outrageous. Luckily, I decided to give him a small challenge to prove himself. Next thing I knew, I was shaking hands with some of the biggest celebrities in the world! All because I gave one guy with a crazy claim a chance.
- A taxi driver once asked what was wrong with me. I almost wanted to tell him to pull over so I could get out – I didn't want to be forced to talk. After all, what would this taxi driver know about my troubles? As it turns out, he became one of my closest confidants and advisors. He even helped me through the hardest time in my life!
- A goofy, lanky, awkward person once approached me to tell me they had a major breakthrough in online marketing. My initial reaction was to shrug this person off, but something about him made me curious enough to ask him what he was talking about. Asking that one question led to a business partnership that generated over $15 million in sales and helped thousands of people in the process.

The list goes on and on in my life.

The bottom line is that, when you meet someone, take a moment to *really* meet them. Be open to them and pay attention to what they say. Don't focus on what their immediate value to your life is - think bigger than that. There are so many scenarios that could play out in the future.

- Perhaps you can be of service to them and it ends there. It's a chance to get some good karma points in life.
- Perhaps they know someone else that they could connect you to (this is almost a guarantee).
- Maybe they don't talk the way you think someone should, but they truly are geniuses.
- Maybe one day you post something on Facebook and they share what you post and that share leads to a huge connection.

The possibilities are endless.

There's almost no risk to keeping an open mind and approaching everyone you ever meet with no assumptions. However, the risk on the other side is huge. If you're constantly vetting every single hand you shake, you're guaranteed to miss out on some amazing connections in your life.

In the end, don't make assumptions - simply make connections. Focus on the core goal of growing your network. It doesn't really matter who you're adding to it as long as they aren't toxic - just keep adding.

The returns will speak for themselves.

Think of Every Handshake As An Interview

I'll let you in on the greatest secret I have for finding the best business partners, team members, and even professional friends.

Ready?

Years ago, I remember listening to an audiobook where the speaker said, "Treat every handshake as an interview."

When I heard this, I was blown away - it sounded incredibly wise. I didn't quite know what he meant, but I immediately started to practice. What I found was that it completely changed the way that I talk to someone when I first meet them.

Actually, the change was that I stopped talking altogether. I focused only on one thing: asking questions.

If I was asked a question, I would reply for the sake of conversation, but I've made a conscious effort to always focus on the other person when I meet someone new.

I find now that I'm mesmerized by people. If you take a minute to just stop talking and start listening, you'll discover how amazing people truly are. The wide array of life experiences, the connections they have, the things they've achieved - it's amazing to hear.

So, I focus on asking questions like...

- Where did you go to school?
- Where did you grow up?
- What do you do right now? Are you a student or working?
- How did you get into that line of work?
- How do you like living in [insert name of city]?
- What do you think about [insert a topic they'll be interested in]?

These are all questions I use to start a conversation.

You'll be surprised how eager most people are to talk about themselves. Then, the trick is to listen - really listen. The follow-up questions should be guided by their responses. Ask deeper questions and really analyze how your conversation is going.

So, why do we do this?

It's simple.

Through asking questions and listening, I end up learning a lot about someone:

- What are their specific skills and talents? Are they great golfers or are they great at the piano? It's all good conversation.
- What are they looking for in life? Are they happy right now?
- What do they need to help them move to the next step?
- Do I have a connection for them?
- Who do they know? What kinds of people are they connected to?
- What do they enjoy doing for fun?

The list is endless.

It's through these questions that I am able to, later on, go and find my best business partners, team members, and friends. By treating every handshake as an interview, I find that I learn a lot about everyone I meet, and that empowers me with information on how to take that connection further.

So, talk less, listen more.

Two People Removed

I have a friend named Jon Talarico, and he taught me a valuable lesson in life. Of all the people I've met over the years —and I've met thousands— I've never met anyone better than Jon at networking and getting his foot in absolutely any, and I mean any, door.

He teaches a concept that he calls *Two People Removed*, and it directly proves why you should be building your network all the time. The key to this concept? Once your network gets big enough, you'll ALWAYS be just two people away from anyone you want to meet in your life.

Trust me, it works!

I've sat down and challenged Jon to his face to test it. The first person I chose was Bill Gates. After just a minute, I realized how I truly am only two people removed from Bill Gates. Next, I tried the Dalai Lama - I was two people removed. I found out that I'm even just two people removed from the President of the United States.

Jon teaches that you can access people quickly if you have a network that knows them. So, going back to the original question that started this entire chapter:

"How do you have such an amazing team and how do you know so many important people?"

The answer is simple.

I know someone in my network who's connected to the person that I want to meet, and they make an introduction. That's it.

If you want to be wealthier, more powerful or more connected - just meet more people and **grow your network.**

Question Time

Once again, it's time for you to see where you stand in terms of how much you focus on your network. To do that, here are some questions to answer:

1. Have you ever seen someone and chosen not to talk to them because of how they were dressed, how they spoke or some other similar reason?
Be honest. Have you ever made a decision to NOT speak to someone because of an external factor that you saw in them?

2. Estimate how many millionaires you know right now...
This needs to be a direct contact. Someone you actually know. Someone who's in your cell phone. How many millionaires do you estimate? Is it between zero and five? Is it five to 10? Is it 15-20? Is it 25+?

3. Have you ever gone out of your way to ask someone to introduce you to someone?
This is such a BIG one! If there's one thing in my life I'm good at, this is it. This might be something as simple as asking one of your friends to

introduce you to one of their friends. It's a skill that you will have to fine tune and become very good at because it's one of the most powerful things you can do.

By now, you should have a good feel for the network you have and what you need to do to grow it. With that idea firmly established, we need to address a problem that you will likely run into.

The more you grow your network, the more you're going to find "negative" people sneaking into your network.

So, what exactly should we do with the negative people in our lives?

CHAPTER 29:
NEGATIVE PEOPLE AND
WHAT TO DO WITH THEM

*"Most people aren't negative to hurt you,
they're negative to protect you."*
– Anik Singal

"Everything in my life sucks. I'm doomed."

This was a conversation I had a few years ago with a friend of mine. On the call, he told me he was going through a really tough time. Although it truly was a hard time for him, everything he said, felt, and thought was 100% negative.

The entire conversation was incredibly doom and gloom.

However, that wasn't what worried me. What worried me was what I felt after I hung up the phone. Before the call, I felt great! I was super happy and excited about what was happening in my life.

But after the call? My first thought was, "Wow. Life *does* suck!"

It took me the rest of the day to look inwards and turn my perception back around to being positive.

Just as I was starting to feel positive again, I got *another* message. That same friend wanted to get on another call to run some ideas by me. Unfortunately, I fell for the call and spent another hour listening to him talk about how unfair the world was to him.

He was spewing negativity!

The negativity wasn't directed at me. It was just general negativity about the world and the people in it. However, his general negativity was still having a huge impact on my mindset.

After that second call, I remember thinking, *"Man. Every time I talk to this person, I always end up feeling horrible for the rest of the day."*

That day really made me realize how much control we have over our own environment. Taking those calls was a *choice* that I made, so I was actually responsible for letting that negativity impact me.

Once I realized that, I started thinking about what I was willing to do to make sure that my environment always stayed positive.

What I found changed my life.

Negativity Is Contagious

Negativity is incredibly contagious.

The worst part is that negativity doesn't require you to be physically present to pass on the germ. Heck, it was spreading to me over the phone!

Even though I felt great just minutes before I got on the call, my mindset shifted dramatically as soon as I started talking with my friend. It didn't matter that nothing he said applied to my life. It didn't matter that everything was going well for me at the time.

That's the crazy thing about negativity. It's contagious to the point of not making any sense.

Even if you're in a good place in your life or mind, you can't let your guard down to those around you who have a negative attitude. Protecting your environment is a full-time job.

It has nothing to do with what is going on in *your* life; it all depends on what is happening in the lives of those *around* you.

Having said all this, let me be very clear. I am not saying that you should just cut the negative people from your life. I am also not saying that you should stop supporting those around you when they need help.

I'm simply saying to evaluate each situation individually.

- Perhaps limiting the conversations with certain people.
- Maybe not sharing too many details with certain people.
- Perhaps limiting contact with certain people who tend to spread their negativity when they're feeling down.

My point is that negativity will creep into your life more often than you would like due to its contagious nature. Knowing that, you need to be fully prepared to manage the negativity around you.

Managing Negative People

Again, you do NOT have to eject these negative people from your life. You might not have many people left in your life if you do that. Instead, you just have to learn to *manage* them.

That's exactly what I did with my friend. I just took a break from him.

Although I wanted to support him, I knew that I wasn't helping. He was using me to vent his frustrations, but I couldn't be that person for him on a daily basis.

So, I put myself first and decided to control the situation.

The next time he wanted a phone call, I courteously turned down the invitation because I was very busy with other things in my life. I had to do this more than a few times, and it was difficult. However, I knew that protecting myself and my environment was the most important thing.

While it may sound like I was not being a supportive friend, I never completely shut him out. Instead, I expressed to him that I was at a very key point in my life and needed to limit my calls so that I could focus. I then asked him to email me his ideas so that I could reply when the time was appropriate for me.

By switching to email, I noticed that he would send me his ideas with none of the negative emotional baggage attached. The negativity only seemed to come out when we had a back and forth conversation on the phone.

This way, we were both winning:

Me: I was protecting myself from the negativity virus.

My friend: He was able to get insightful feedback and advice from me on his ideas that would actually help him!

We followed this formula for a few weeks, and he never once felt offended.

I realized that most of the people around you are happy to comply when you give them certain guidelines for communication. By working with him through email, he got the support he needed and I was able to keep my positive mindset.

Things eventually began to change for him, and his mood completely turned once good things started happening again. He went from being negative to laughing, smiling, and joking around again. Once I saw this, I was able to let my guard down around him a bit.

Notice that I never had to cut him from my life.

Instead, I changed the way I associated and interacted with him. I set up a *buffer* between us so that I didn't have to bear the brunt of his negativity.

When we talk about negativity, so many people think that we're talking about people who are negative toward *you* specifically. That's NOT true. It means the people who are negative in general.

The people who are negative about YOU represent a whole different ball game.

Yes, these people exist and also need to be managed.

These are the people who seem to love putting down your dream or your vision. They repeatedly tell you that you're crazy. They harp on you. They warn you to stop. Some even flat out tell you they don't believe that you can accomplish something.

I thought that people would stop doing this once I started experiencing success in my ventures.

Unfortunately, that hasn't been the case at all.

Actually, a very dear friend of mine tried to talk me out of a key dream. This particular friend had always been supportive. He had helped me through some of the worst times of my life.

What's more is we've made millions of dollars together working on different projects.

So, it was clear that this person wished me no harm. However, this friend called me at a time when I was making a life-changing decision and said, "Anik, what you're doing is stupid. You'll ruin yourself. Don't do it."

I was stunned.

He made his opinion very clear to me. He told me that I was going to fail in my venture and that he had no faith in my idea.

Now, imagine if someone you respect calls up you to tell you that your dream is a massive mistake and it will ruin your life. What would you do? Most people would probably take it serious and say, "You're right! I'm not going to do it."

Trust me, his words had a huge impact on me - I almost quit. However, I remembered one of my CORE rules in life: *only take advice from those who have actually done what you're trying to do.* My friend had zero experience with the journey on which I was about to embark. If he didn't believe that he could do it, how could he believe that I could do it?

So, is it possible that this friend was not even being negative in their own mind? Is it possible that he was being PROTECTIVE? Absolutely! I recognized that at the time and though I didn't take his advice, I appreciated his attempt to protect me. I went forward and launched the project I wanted to do.

So, what happened?

It turned out to the be the single best thing I've ever done in my career. So, remember that many people act in seemingly negative ways toward you because they're trying to protect you from yourself. Their own belief patterns are going to drive what they think is possible for you.

Always take the advice that you get with a grain of salt and evaluate who and where it's coming from!

Learning The Triggers

To effectively manage a relationship with someone who is negative, you need to learn more about their triggers. Yes, this means that you need to get good at reading people and picking up their state of mind.

Most of us are not tuned into others at all times. Initially, it may even feel tough. However, it becomes a natural state with enough practice.

If you study the people around you, you're going to realize one thing about human beings:

All humans work in patterns. They all have triggers and reactions that can be predicted.

Learn to tune into these patterns to help you better manage the environment you create around yourself. This way, you can immediately make changes whenever someone starts being negative in general or negative toward you specifically.

If someone is being negative in general - try to immediately limit your exposure to it. You can still support them, but it is always okay to put yourself first and support them in a way that will protect you as well.

If someone is being negative toward you specifically - just thank them for their advice and take ownership over what you share with them and what you don't. Perhaps certain things you're doing or talking about are triggering their negativity.

Moving forward, just avoid those conversations with them.

Question Time

Now that you have a good idea of what it means to have negative people in your life, here are a few questions to answer:

1. The last time someone told you that you couldn't do something, how did you react?
Did it end in an argument or did you realize that it was just their opinion?

2. Are you too busy trying to convince those around you to think like you?
Are you using your energy for this or are you using that energy to go out and fight for your dreams? After all, you have a limited amount of energy in any given day.

3. Is there anyone that you talk to regularly who seems to always have a negative outlook on life?
I want you to journal this and think very hard about it. Are there people in your life that make you feel worse rather than better after spending time with them?

You have to make a list of those people right away so you can learn to manage their presence in your life. Remember, you don't have to delete them. You just need to learn to own the environment that you allow them to create.

Now that you have a solid idea of how to manage the negative people in your life, let's talk about the positive ones. There are likely hundreds - yes, I said hundreds - of people around you that would be happy to help you.

The only issue is that you never give them a chance to help!

In the next chapter, I want to talk about how important it is to always ask questions.

CHAPTER 30:
ASK QUESTIONS, SEEK ANSWERS

"Ask for help not because you are weak
but because you want to remain strong."
– Les Brown

When I was starting my Entrepreneurial journey back in 2003, I had a lot of questions. I didn't have anyone to guide me, so I relied on the online forum that I had found.

If you know me at all, it should come as no surprise that the members of that forum came to refer to me as the "annoying kid" because of all of the questions I asked.

Most people would hate being called annoying, but I actually wear the title with great pride.

Here's why...

As I was searching around on Google, I discovered this online forum that finally felt "legit" to me. There were tons of people on there making money online. They would help one another, reveal strategies, and give lots of great tips.

Naturally, I started spending HOURS on this forum every single day and didn't hold back from asking any questions that came to mind.

Thinking back, I'm actually amazed at myself. I never wasted time. Even when people would poke fun at me and call me the "annoying kid" - I never let it slow me down. The only thing I was focused on was getting my answers, period.

I also realized very early in life that time was precious. It didn't make sense spending days making mistakes and dealing with headaches when I could avoid it all by just asking someone who already knew the answer!

It's now 15 years later and nothing has changed. I am not the least bit shy to ask questions, to ask for help. I'm constantly seeking out experts and leaning on them in a respectful way that helps both of us.

The key takeaway is that my ego never stops me. I'm never embarrassed. I don't sweat the little things. My focus stays solely on one thing: getting reliable, accurate, and fast answers.

The Need For Fast Answers

One of the biggest things I've learned in life is the value of getting fast answers.

The concept is actually very simple.

Why would anyone spend countless hours or days trying to figure something out when they can simply ask an expert and get an answer in five minutes?

On the surface, it sounds like common sense, right? However, many people avoid asking questions for several reasons...

1. *"I'll look stupid."*
   So what? First of all, this rarely happens. How many times has someone asked you for help and your immediate reaction was, *"Wow. This person is pretty stupid."* Probably not often. This is just an unreasonable fear we have. Even if they do think you're stupid, who cares what they think? At least you got your answer.

2. *"I don't want to bother them."*
   Now, of course there are limits to everything. If you're asking someone for help on a daily basis and disrupting their life, you're overstepping your boundaries. But, within reason, this is usually a false belief that you'll need to get over. You have a wide circle and can always balance who you ask for help. Also, remember that most people actually love being called on for help. In a way, you're showing them great respect by honoring their knowledge.

3. *"I want to figure it out on my own."*
   Sometimes this a good thing to do. The journey of searching for an answer can teach you a lot, but I honestly don't bother with this journey most of the time. I believe in momentum and speed, so I don't want to waste time. If you're having a lot of *I can do it on my own* moments, really evaluate your ego. Ask yourself if it's getting in the way of your own success.

In the end, I feel that nothing is more important than my dream and mission. So, wasting time dealing with my fears, feelings, and ego is not an option.

When you're stuck, always remember to ask yourself, "How much time is this particular obstacle really worth?"

My Facebook Account

My family has this joke about my Facebook account. They make fun of me and say all I use Facebook for is to post job openings or ask people for suggestions, references, or answers.

I chuckle right along with them because, well, it's true.

I post job openings, reference checks, and requests for referrals all the time to my personal Facebook account. Why wouldn't I? I'm connected with over 2,000 brilliant people.

I can honestly say there isn't a single question I have that one of these 2,000 people won't have an answer to. There isn't a single person in the world that I need to meet that one of them can't introduce me to.

So, why wouldn't I deploy my network when I need them? I've made some amazing things happen because of a simple 30-second Facebook post...

1. I found Lurn's head of operations.
2. I made a multi-million dollar joint venture.
3. I even met someone who helped me make my dream of getting a TEDx talk come true.

The list goes on.

So, even if you're anxious about asking someone for help face to face, how about taking 30 seconds and putting out posts on social media?

You'll be amazed at what comes back when you just take a moment to ask.

Henry Ford's Famous Rant

In 1916, the Chicago Tribune published an article insulting Henry Ford, essentially calling him an idiot. They went so far as to say that he was, "Incapable of thought."

Ford was not happy about this accusation and sued them for $1 million. In court, the defense attorney decided to make a point by asking Henry Ford question after question about American history and other trivial matters.

Ford got question after question wrong. He was laughed at. He was ridiculed. His wrong answers were written about all over the newspapers. However, he won the hearts of everyone by making a simple statement:

> *"If I should really want to answer the foolish question you have just asked, or any of the other questions you have been asking me, let me remind you that I have a row of electric push-buttons on my desk.*
>
> *And by pushing the right button, I can summon to my aid men who can answer any question I desire to ask concerning the business to which I am devoting most of my efforts.*
>
> *Now, will you kindly tell me, why I should clutter up my mind with general knowledge, for the purpose of being able to answer questions, when I have men around me who can supply any knowledge I require?"*

I remember learning about this case in 10th grade. I can still remember where I was sitting when the teacher told us this story. It had a huge impact on me back then and continues to drive how I think today.

Basic conclusion?

You're better off surrounding yourself with those who have all the answers rather than wasting time trying to become the one who has all the answers.

Asking questions just may be a secret that many of the world's billionaires are exploiting to this very day. If they are, why aren't you?

Question Time

Now, let's see just how good you are at asking questions...

1. Are you afraid to text someone and ask them a question?
Do you feel like you will be bothering them? Do you feel stupid asking? Do you generally shy away from asking someone for help?

2. Would you rather spend a day researching something to find the answer yourself or just ask someone?
Be honest here. What is your natural inclination? Do you lean toward sitting around and Googling forever or do you prefer to reach out to someone who knows the answer?

3. Have you ever posted a request or question on social media?
Have you ever genuinely asked a question or looked for a solution on social media? Have you put yourself out there to those who know you and said, "I don't know the answer to this. Can somebody help me?"

The biggest objection I get to asking questions typically is, "Anik, I don't have anyone who I can ask questions to in my life." Although I don't believe for even a moment that this is true, the final element of Stage 4 will address this too.

It's time you found an official mentor...

CHAPTER 31:
MENTORSHIP

"A mentor is someone who sees more talent and ability within you, than you see in yourself, and helps bring it out of you."
– Bob Proctor

There are two types of mentors in life - you need both.

1. The God-Given (your parents or guardians)
2. The Chosen (those you ask to teach you)

The very first mentors I ever had were my mother and father.

These wonderful people taught me that impossible is nothing more than an opinion and that we can ALWAYS be better. They also taught me the meaning of true love.

I cannot begin to tell you how important these lessons are in today's world. There is no skill or talent you can learn that can match the power of knowing unconditional love.

No one thing in your life will impact your wealth or success as much as love.

My mother was the one who taught me absolute selfless love. I grew up watching her pour herself out to us without ever wanting a single thing in return. Many times we didn't even know the sacrifices she would make for us because she would never mention them.

Today, I can look back and see that sacrificing for others is a skill that I learned from the very best mentor I could have.

My father taught me that *impossible is only an opinion.*

Sometimes, when people tell me how much I've achieved, I laugh inside because it feels so small in comparison to what my father achieved. Growing up in a small village in India, his home didn't even have electricity.

My grandfather wanted my father to study hard and become a top-notch engineer, but he had to curl up near candles or use the street lamp just to study.

Today, he holds a head engineering position with the Nuclear Regulatory Commission in the United States Government.

He rose to the top ranks in India, brought his family to the United States and provided his children with every luxury and opportunity one could dream of. So, yes, when he was sitting under that candle in a tiny village that was barely on the map - I have no doubt that he understood that *impossible is only an opinion.*

These two lessons alone have led me to where I am today. I've had mentors from the day I was born and I've always cherished their role in my life. Even to this day, I make sure I have a mentor for every key area in my life.

I'm constantly finding people who are more talented or experienced than I am and asking them to guide me.

Are You Coachable?

"Do you REALLY want to learn this? Are you going to be coachable?"

These were the exact words of the first professional mentor I ever had in my life, Solomon Evangelista. Solomon was the marketing director at a financial planning company I joined as an independent contractor. Back then, I was a truly shy, reserved, and scared person. I wanted to learn business, but even the thought of making a presentation or "selling" scared me into paralysis.

As life would have it, Solomon had other plans for me. Lucky for me, my father had made sure that I was an incredibly coachable person.

As I started working through my assignments, I had one that said I had to book an appointment with a potential client and go to their home to make a presentation. Booking the appointment was no problem. It was the fear that came over me after booking the appointment which was the problem.

I remember running to Solomon's office and saying, "I need your help. I can't do this on my own. Can you teach me what to do?"

I still remember his reaction. He slowly looked up at me with a very firm face and asked me those two questions, "Do you REALLY want to learn this? Are you going to be coachable?"

My reaction was pure confusion, so he clarified what he was asking:

"Are you going to be coachable? Are you going to do what I tell you to do? Are you going to listen and implement? Or are you going to argue and think that you know everything?"

And all I said was, "Solomon, why would I ask you for advice if I didn't plan on listening and doing it?"

His answer?

"I don't know. You tell me. Because most people ask but never listen."

That was the day that Solomon proved to me that being coachable was not common sense or a natural occurrence.

It's actually a choice.

Being Coachable Is A Choice

When you choose to be coachable, you're putting your faith in someone else. Even more than that, you're openly accepting that they know more than you about certain topics. You're accepting that you don't know it all. You're accepting that you may be asked to do things that are uncomfortable. When you ask someone to coach you, you're committing to do whatever they tell you to (within ethical and moral limits, of course).

Bob Proctor once told me something that stuck with me. He said, "So many want to be taught, but they want to tell you how to teach them." Now, after having taught over 250,000 students in my life, I can tell you - without a shadow of doubt - how true this statement is.

Most people like the "idea" of being coached or mentored, but the minute they're told to do something uncomfortable or scary, they become a ball of excuses. There's no greater way to dishonor a mentor's time than to ignore their teachings, argue with their experience or, even worse, waste their time with complaining.

So, before you ever go seeking a mentor, you need to have a very serious conversation with yourself.

1. Are you willing to put your ego aside and actually listen?
2. Are you open to being stretched and made uncomfortable?
3. Will you willing to try new things even if it's the opposite of what you've done in the past?
4. Are you going to be accountable and place urgency on what you're taught by your mentor?

Having a mentor is important, but being in a place where you can truly be open to the mentor is even more important. Remember that true mentors are not typically in it *for the money*. Most of them have succeeded in their life (a key part of choosing the right mentor), so they're mentoring as a way of giving back.

A great mentor really just wants to see you succeed. They want to see their impact. So, the biggest compensation you can provide a mentor is to actually take action on their advice.

Having a mentor is amazing and a true blessing, but by no means is it easy. A great mentor will stretch you and consistently pull you out of your comfort zone.

I mean, that's kind of the point, right?

I have no idea where I would be today without the mentors I've had. I can easily count over 10 mentors that have worked with me in the last 15 years alone, teaching me incredibly vital skills.

- Learning to speak in front of thousands of people - taught by a mentor.
- Writing copy that generates millions of dollars - taught by a mentor.
- Scaling my company - coached by a mentor.
- Leading a life-changing non-profit initiative in India - guided by a mentor.
- Losing weight and getting healthier - you guessed it, mentor.

Whether it's my personal life or professional life, I have always surrounded myself with mentors.

Now, you may ask why I have had so many. Why 10 mentors in just 15 years?

I've had so many because I believe that every mentor has their own place in my life. It's not uncommon to outgrow your need for a specific mentor. Just because someone is a good mentor for you in one season of your life doesn't necessarily mean that will hold true in another season.

There have been times when I simply outgrew the advice of my mentor. There have been times when I truly learned everything I could from a mentor, and it was time to fine-tune a different skill set. There were even times where the relationship just didn't work out the way either of us thought that it would.

The point I'm trying to make is that choosing a mentor doesn't necessarily have to be a lifetime decision. Always be prepared to analyze the coaching you're getting and the results it's getting you.

I'm very strategic with the coaching and mentorship I get.

I have mentors in both my personal life and my professional life, and I've even had times when I had multiple mentors in each - it all just depends on where I am in my life and what I need.

So, the most important takeaway is that you need to determine in which part of your life you want a mentor. You need to really ask yourself if you're truly prepared to be open to someone else's direction.

So, let's see if you really are...

Question Time

And now to see how coachable *you* are:

1. Are you coachable or are you a difficult person?
I really want you to take time to answer this. Really think about it and know that most people are not coachable. For the most part, we are naturally *not* coachable. It's a skill you have to choose to learn.

2. Do you seek advice from people who shouldn't be giving you advice?
This is such a great question. Remember, you can't ask an engineer how to perform surgery and you can't ask a surgeon how to design a machine.

3. Do you currently have someone in your life who is your mentor?
If you aren't sure, think of it this way - when I say the word mentor, is there an image or a name that pops into your mind?

The answers to these three questions will really help you understand where you are in the mentorship part of your life.

And that is the end of Stage 4—People.

It's been quite the journey.

The greatest realization we can have at the end of Stage 4 is just how much of a commitment it takes to truly succeed as an Entrepreneur. It's not as easy as some make it sound. It takes more than having a conversation in your mind and saying, "*I want my own business.*"

There's work to be done!

Let's quickly summarize and then talk about what's next.

CHAPTER 32:
NEXT STEPS

"When Life Pushes you stand straight,
smile and push it the heck back."
– Anik Singal

And here we are.

It's been quite the journey, hasn't it?

First, I want to thank you for having the faith, trust and belief in my ability to help you unlock the inner workings of an Entrepreneurial mind. I want you to know that I realize the weight of the responsibility you given to me.

After all, unleashing the incredible Entrepreneur within you could be one of the most defining actions of your life. Your dreams, your goals, and your ability to influence this world with your legacy - it all starts with unlocking the Entrepreneurial code.

I wrote this book precisely because I wish someone had handed me these guidelines two decades ago when I started my own journey. Unfortunately, I had no choice but to turn to the system that was in front of me.

Succeeding as an Entrepreneur only happened because I FOUGHT the system, not because I followed it. You can have the same success and I want you to understand that myself and the entire #LurnNation is standing right behind you.

We have your back.

No matter what anyone teaches, remember that becoming a successful Entrepreneur may have a simple code, but it's far from easy. An Entrepreneur's journey is a lifelong one. We will never even come close to achieving perfection.

As we grow, the challenges we face will grow too. The obstacles will adapt to our growth, but our impact will also escalate. This isn't a bad thing at all - growth challenges are exactly how you know you're on the right path.

Just think - even the most successful billionaires still spend countless hours reading books, taking courses and working with consultants. No matter what level of success any of them have achieved, they keep their aim on learning and growing.

As long as you remember that becoming an Entrepreneur is a journey and not a destination, nothing can stop you.

We're Not Part Of The "System"

Whether you're an Entrepreneur or an Intrapreneur, always remember that we aren't part of the traditional system. When we were in school and they asked us what we wanted to be when we grew up, there was never a box we could check with the word Entrepreneur next to it.

The system isn't set up to build Entrepreneurs. As a matter of fact, it's quite the opposite. But remember that the system was established decades, if not centuries ago, and it simply is losing application today.

Our lives have been designed from the day we're born to do one thing: please others. Our limits...defined by others. Our capabilities...defined by others. Our possibilities...defined by others. Our dreams and goals...controlled by others.

But it stops here.

If you ever need to be reminded of whether you can truly succeed as an Entrepreneur, just take a few moments to watch a toddler. Pay attention to how they constantly explore everything around them. Observe how they're determined to find answers themselves and never wait around for anyone's help. Observe how curious and *persistent* a child can be.

Remind yourself that that is exactly who you were. That toddler is exactly how you started. That persistence, that curiosity, that independence, and that spirit were all God's gift to you. All you need to do is re-awaken that side of you, because we often part ways with that type of thinking.

We start getting told "no." Soon after that, we enter school and are told what to do, when to do it and how to do it. Before we know it, we have to score well on standardized tests just to impress some admission officers who will never meet us or know who we really are.

Even if you were admitted to a university you would just start the cycle again to impress a recruiter to hire you. At your job, the cycle would endlessly repeat as you try to impress our boss - all for a promotion.

That's exactly what the system is designed to teach. Nowhere in that system is an Entrepreneur or an Intrapreneur considered a viable path. That ends now.

No matter how long you were in the system, it's absolutely possible to escape.

You already have what it takes.

What Does Your eSCORE Say?

Speaking of the next steps, it's imperative you take the eSCAPE quiz inside #LurnNation. It's 100% free, and it will provide you with amazing insight on where you should focus your training.

The eSCORE quiz is designed to delve deep into your mind to learn about who you are as an Entrepreneur. Our goal from the eSCORE quiz isn't to determine what your future holds, but rather what you need in your life to unlock your potential.

You'll start with getting an understanding of where you are on the *Entrepreneurial scale,* but the part that comes after is the most important - it's the part that dissects your scores by each Stage.

Stage #1 – Self
Stage #2 – Catapult
Stage #3 – Authority
Stage #4 – People

Before you make assumptions, take the quiz. You may be very surprised what parts are your strongest and what parts are your weakest.

I highly recommend you take the quiz today, work on your strengths and weaknesses and then return every few months to take the quiz again. You'll be able to track your progress and growth as an Entrepreneur.

To see the quiz, go to: www.Lurn.com/quiz.

Mastering The 4-Stage Journey...

Here's a question I was asked the first time I ever presented the eSCAPE formula. I thought it was great, so I wanted to include it here as we wrap up:

"Anik, do we have to go in order from Stage #1 to #2 to #3 to #4? I'm finding my Stage #2 is weaker than Stage #3. What do I do?"

My answer to that question is that most people will find themselves going in order from #1 to #4. However, it's not absolutely necessary to do that. Remember, it's not about the order of the steps, but rather the steps themselves.

Everyone's Entrepreneurial journey is different. We are impacted by our environments, our upbringing, our success, our challenges, our friends and so much more. So many things shape who we are that there will never be two people on this journey in the same exact place.

Hence, it's absolutely possible that you may have to work on your Authority Stage before you work on your Catapult stage. The order means very little compared to having each Stage mastered.

This is exactly why I recommend using the eSCORE to help guide where you focus your energy. Whatever you do, pick one characteristic, focus on it and never stop improving who you are.

What if you just can't handle a stage or a key element? What if it's too hard even after a lot of trying?

Remember, nothing worth having can be done alone. If there is any stage or characteristic that just isn't happening for you - all hope is not lost.

Your goal will be to learn about your weaknesses so you can build a team around you to strengthen your weaknesses. Period.

Again, the gift here is that you get a chance to learn exactly what and who you need in your life to up your Entrepreneurial game.

WHAT'S NEXT IN OUR JOURNEY TOGETHER? #LURNNATION - JOIN US TODAY

The bottom line is that, if you truly want to succeed as an Entrepreneur, you need to make a daily conscious effort to...

- Keep learning...
- Keep networking...
- Keep practicing...

This was one of the hardest things about becoming an Entrepreneur for me - I craved having that community, a community that would *have my back*. It became my personal obsession to make sure that no Entrepreneur ever had this problem again.

One of the greatest joys of my life is hearing from our students, engaging with them and interacting with them. We're always here to support you, so please feel free to connect with us in any of the following ways.

#1 - FREE Account at #LurnNation

I'm so excited to invite you today to join our #LurnNation community at www.Lurn.com. We're a worldwide community of Entrepreneurs and fighters who are committed to our dreams. We have thousands of members from almost every country you can imagine.

It's 100% free to create your account and join us. We have countless free courses in the community and much, much more. I promise that you'll never regret taking 30 seconds to create your account and get engaged.

#2 - Visit Us at The Lurn Center

We have a physical home for you to visit where we offer workshops, many of which are absolutely free. If you want to learn more about joining us, please go to www.LurnCenter.com to find all of the details that you'll need. It truly is the Transformational Home for Entrepreneurs.

#3 - Come Talk To Me on Social Media!

I try my best to be active on the following networks and social media:

Facebook: www.Facebook.com/AnikSingalcom
Instagram: @singalanik
YouTube: www.YouTube.com/aniksingalcom
Website: www.Lurn.com & www.AnikSingal.com
Podcast: www.AnikSingal.com/podcast

I'll be the first to admit I could be quicker on adopting social media, but I'm slowly adding more and more every month. Just visit my website - www.AnikSingal.com - to keep in touch and up to date with what I'm doing!

#4 - Check Out My eSCAPE Masterclass!

Due to high demand, I've decided to run a masterclass called eSCAPE. This is a coaching program attached directly to what I teach in this book. We go through each part of the book one step at a time with guided exercises to help you up your Entrepreneurial skills.

To learn more, please go to www.Lurn.com/emaster.

We have a lot of fun in this group of crazy Entrepreneurs, so please feel free to join me!

Whatever You Do - Never, Ever Give Up...

I'm emotional as I write the last paragraphs of this book. Thank you again for your faith in my ability to help you become a better Entrepreneur. Always know that I'm here for you in any way that I can be.

I'll leave you with my thoughts about you becoming an Entrepreneur...

Always be intentional, on a daily basis, about growing as an Entrepreneur. Face your challenges as if they are blessings. Fight for your dreams, and let nothing overtake or overrule your mission in life.

If you ever doubt that you can do it remember, I personally devoted my life to helping people simply because I KNOW that you can do it.

You have everything at your fingertips. You have all the support you need. Now, just go out there and do it. The world awaits your impact, your dreams await your arrival and, most of all, we at Lurn Nation await your amazing success story.

Never ever give up. Take it off the table. Never. Ever. Give. Up. Period.

Finally, always remember…

"When life pushes you, stand straight, smile and push it the heck back!"